RECLAI
SACRED
PATH

To Cheryl,

With Brightest Blessings,

"Jon is the master Sage taking a reader on a journey of their own self-discovery. Through his own story of personal transformation, Jon now shares the tools he has learned and made in order to help shape your own sacred path. Through both wit and wisdom, Jon guides you to knowing the deeper level of your soul's purpose. Each chapter allows a reader to begin to develop and practice skills under Jon's careful mentorship. One becomes clearer and focused progressing through each level of understanding."

—Eileen Dey, Founder of The Reiki Training Program

RECLAIMING *your* SACRED PATH

Using Divination,
Manifestation, and Healing
to Resume Your Spiritual Journey

JON MARTIN ANASTASIO

TURNING
STONE
PRESS

Reclaiming Your Sacred Path

Reclaiming Your Sacred Path:
Using Divination, Manifestation, and Healing to
Resume Your Spiritual Journey
Jon Martin Anastasio

Cover design by Frame25 Productions
Cover art © Nik Niklz c/o Shutterstock.com
Interior design by Frame25 Productions

Turning Stone Press
8301 Broadway Street, Suite 219
San Antonio, TX 78209
www.turningstonepress.com

Library of Congress Control Number available upon request

ISBN 978-1-61852-108-8

10 9 8 7 6 5 4 3 2 1

Printed in the United States of America

This book is dedicated to the rebirth of joy, wonder, and fulfillment among those who have come to believe that what they see and hear every day is all there is.

I am grateful to Kelly Lynn Glab because without her love, support and encouragement this book might not have seen the light of day.

I give special thanks to my daughter Ali, a courageous soul who has been true to her path for so many years, and to my daughter, Abby and my son, Danny, who throughout their lives have continually reminded me that there is so much more than meets the eye.

I have had the good fortune to be inspired, coached, led, mentored and taught by some extraordinary people. I am grateful to Eileen Dey Wurst, Reiki Master and Teacher and Founder of Seattle's Reiki Training Program; to the Reverend Donald Lewis, First Priest and Chancellor of the Correllian Nativist Tradition, whose life of service and immense body of creative work has helped and inspired so many; and to my personal mentors and teachers along the path—Lady Windy LaJoie, Rev. John Snodgrass, and Lady Anna Rowe.

Brightest Blessings and thanks to you all.

"*The Fool, a Major Arcanum that indicates the importance of trusting in our own judgment—even if others may think us foolish. Often the Fool is shown in the act of walking off the side of a cliff— an act that anyone would consider foolish. Yet the moral of the card is that—as in the cartoons—the Fool will not fall unless he looks down. That is, all will be well as long as we do not doubt ourselves.*"

—Rev. Donald Lewis-Highcorrell, Chancellor, Correllian Nativist Tradition of Wicca

CONTENTS

Author's Preface   xiii

PART ONE: Discovering a New Spiritual Path

1. Resuming the Journey   3
2. Your Spiritual Autonomy   9
3. The Courage to Change   17
4. The Power and Healing Framework
   for Learning and Growth   37
5. Centering for Power and Healing   41

PART TWO: Gaining Insight for Resuming Your Journey by Using Divination, Manifestation, and Healing

6. An Introduction to Divination   55
7. Using Futhark Runes for Divination   67
8. The Tarot   83
9. Manifestation: Focusing and Directing Energy   117
10. Healing   125

PART THREE: Your Spiritual Growth Plan

11. Five Steps to Resuming Your Journey   135
Conclusion   163
Bibliography   169

AUTHOR'S PREFACE

THIS BOOK IS FOR EVERYONE, right now, who experiences the longing in their heart for connection with Spirit; with purpose, who has been on a path that has run out; who has reached a decision point in their life and has no idea where to get guidance for what comes next.

It is also a learning resource for the coaches, guides, and teachers working with students of spirituality. We are skilled in the tools, techniques, and knowledge and in how to impart them, but this book provides a learning process, a way for the seeker or student to come to answer *why* they are embarking on this journey.

It has taken me far too long to remember that I am an autonomous spiritual being, designed to grow and learn and change. I am here to evolve, to reach my Soul's highest potential through connection to my Higher Self and Divine Guidance. And so are you.

If you have any doubt about that, this book is for you.

While we are autonomous, most of our lessons in this life come to us through interaction with other people. I believe we can only come into authentic alignment with others in our lives when we are on the journey to becoming the best of who we are.

I believe in reincarnation. I believe that each time we return, we establish a purpose for the life we are about to live and that the birth process buries that memory in places we cannot access without willingness and effort.

But we get hints and indications. We experience synchronicities, coincidences; we are drawn to—or repelled by—people and places without knowing why. And then we begin to wonder.

We build a life, follow a path (or just our noses), and, suddenly, we awake to the circumstances of our lives. We see multiple possibilities in each decision and choice that crosses our path, and wonder how we got to where we are and what to do next.

This book will help you establish a plan for your current learning journey—your Soul's path to growth—using all the tools and resources at your disposal here in this lifetime.

Because I believe in reincarnation, I began this book with my own Soul's evolution in mind—I wanted to leave a map for my future self so the journey back to Spirit would not be so long and circuitous. Then I began to hear stories that told me I was not alone. I'm still working on integrating all that I've learned so far, but if I wait until I'm done, it will be too late, because when my Soul is done growing in this round, I won't be here anymore. So this is what I've got so far, and I hope it's useful.

I have spent almost forty years working with people in organizations who are seeking to become more creative and effective as leaders, communicators, and team members. It has always been clear to me that the true arena for personal growth is spiritual—the ability to align your mental, physical, and emotional energy with a sense of purpose, no matter what your role or the form your work is taking right now. And it doesn't matter what context or environment we are in when we find each other—we are together for a reason, and that reason has very little to do with the specific circumstances. It is a moment in which the God(dess) in you and the God(dess) in me reach out to each other for learning and growth.

As a Reiki Master, Shamanic Divination facilitator, and magical practitioner, I meet many people who are on a spiritual search but are distressed because they are not making progress and have no idea what to do next. Many would advise them to simply learn to listen to their inner guidance. But they don't know how, they are too anxious to do so, or, in this hyper-connected age, they are too distracted.

So this book is my effort to bring some principles of learning, growth, and change that drive learning and development in organizations to the spiritual journey. If corporations can harness the energy of the universe to create, design, build, and sell billions of dollars worth of product, then individuals can use those same principles to focus and direct energy toward spiritual growth and change for the healing benefit of themselves and others. If we change ourselves, we change the world.

I offer the information in this book as a resource to help you take control of your journey by creating a full and meaningful vision for your spiritual life, defining the principles that will guide you, and beginning to develop the knowledge and skills to get there.

The material in this book is the result of my experience working with thousands of people to apply the best principles of personal growth and change from the behavioral sciences to achieve their goals. And it is also the result of my decades of experience in two major world religions, mindfulness training, Reiki healing and therapeutic touch, stress management, shamanic healing, *A Course in Miracles*, and Wiccan studies. Few ideas here will be wholly new, but I hope the combination and sequence of the information will be helpful in evolving your thinking and making progress in new ways.

Using this book

The book begins by exploring the idea of spiritual autonomy and what it means to you. The chapters that follow explore various spiritual concepts and principles, leading to a three-part framework for moving forward: taking intentional action, reflecting and seeking inner guidance, and energetic healing for the things you discover that must be worked through.

The second section of this book will help you build skills in the Spiritual experiential tools of focusing, centering, and grounding, and in divination (Tarot and Futhark Runes). If you are brand new to the path of Spiritual experience, these will offer a helpful start in accessing your inner wisdom. If you already use divination and know how to focus and direct energy, you can proceed to the work of defining your path to growth, using divination to help you envision it.

Every path begins where you are standing, so you'll answer the first question: What brings you here? Where are you now? Then, you'll move on to the second question: Where are you going? And you will define your vision for your path, the values and principles that guide you, and the capabilities you need to acquire to make it work.

Then, you'll work on resistance—the internal and external factors that can stop you from achieving your vision. I will ask you to revisit your vision after working through this material to ensure you haven't limited your thinking.

Once you've defined where you are and where you're going, and what you need to get there, you will work on building skill in focusing and directing energy—manifestation—through using some fundamental magical working. Again, if you are an adept, please use what you know.

Then you will build your plan.

But that's not the end of this process. There are many reasons that learning and change fail to yield results, but one has stood out for me throughout my experience. When we fail to release the old way of being and try to install the new, we run out of capacity. As you travel this new path, you must leave the old in the rearview mirror. And that requires healing loss and the stresses of the journey.

In the end, you will be on your way. At some point in the future, you may find yourself once again wondering what to do because this plan has run its course.

Pick up the book again. This process is repeatable, as many times as you need it.

PART ONE

Discovering a New Spiritual Path

Chapter One

RESUMING THE JOURNEY

There is no path that goes all the way.
—Han-Shan

IT IS SAID THAT THE most difficult part of a long journey is the first step; however, this can also be true of the first step back along a path we previously thought abandoned or closed to us.

It happens to everyone. Sooner or later, each of us finds we've achieved the goals we set earlier in life, we come to the end of the purpose that drove us, something big falls apart, or we are simply worn out—feeling in need of renewal. The old answers no longer work, and the old structures no longer serve.

Through it all, there is only one thing over which you have complete control—yourself. The personal truth is that you are an autonomous spiritual being. You are free and capable of making your own choices regarding your purpose, your path, and your life. And it is necessary that you do so.

We can wander through practices and enthusiasms, study different forms of spiritual practice to try them on, but most won't stick. You may have figured out that trading spouses, changing jobs, chasing every new metaphysical answer that arises do not solve the problem.

If life's changes are causing you to seek a path back to feeling engaged, powerful, productive, if you are ready for a new beginning, you will need a way to define your vision for what's next, and empower yourself to pursue it, through the methods of divination and manifestation.

There are five key steps to resuming your journey back to purpose: building a vision, defining your values, building your capabilities, building resilience/reducing resistance, and, finally, creating a plan.

By following these five steps, you can prepare yourself to start on that next "first" step on your journey to purpose.

1. Building a Vision

The Fool card in the Major Arcanum in the Tarot deck is usually depicted as about to step off the cliff. In Looney Tunes fashion, though, the Fool will be safe, as long as he does not look down and trusts completely that he is safe. To successfully resume your journey to your purpose, you must become the Fool—innocent, trusting, ready to take that step off the cliff, believing that no harm will befall you if you don't look down.

When we find ourselves at the edge of the cliff, rucksack in hand, we are focused on what we do not want, what we are leaving behind. Anyone familiar with the Law of Attraction will happily explain that if you focus on what you do not want, you will have a clear vision of exactly that in your mind, which will attract more of it to you. Doing what you have always done will get you more of the same. If you don't want *this*, you have to define *that* to exactly the same level of clarity and focus on it to attract it to you.

Your vision affirms what is most important to you and calls you to see it in your life, including seeing the positive actions you will take in the direction of that intention. It is the picture of what you will be doing, the way it will feel, the impact you will have, how you will be of service, how you will worship and connect to the Divine. When you connect to the Divine, you can learn to divine with it in order to receive guidance and counseling along your path. You will find exercises and tools to create the vision for your path in chapter 11.

2. Defining Your Values

For what would you risk everything?

Identifying the things that matter most to you will help you develop a set of guiding principles against which to assess and make decisions about how you will live your life and approach your sacred path. Rather than simply seeking an end to confusion, confirming your values can allow you to endure uncertainty long enough to come up with the answer that is most true for you. Your values help you decide what you will do and what you won't do. On a spiritual level, giving up on what matters most to us hurts far more than whatever may have caused us to do so. Things may be difficult, but being true to yourself and your commitments will always lead you to a better outcome and to growth.

3. Building Your Capabilities

What will it take to make your vision a reality? What are the strengths you can rely on? What capabilities and knowledge do you need to acquire?

The plan for your spiritual journey begins with your vision, your values, and a frank assessment of the extent to which your life currently reflects them. You will explore how to look, ask questions, and connect with the larger part of yourself, to gain insight and direction from the part of you that embarked on this journey in the first place. In the mundane world, that process of questioning and seeking guidance is known as "research." In the spiritual traditions, it is known as divination—and there are many ways to do it, some of which we will explore in later chapters.

Then you have to learn to do something with what you discover. You need to be able to focus and direct energy to make something happen. In the mundane world, this is known as crafting, building, producing, or assembling. In this book, it is called manifestation. So divination and manifestation can be seen as reflection and action. Through divination, you see the reflection of your desires, and through manifestation, you take actions to see them created. This is the cycle through which we learn and grow.

4. Reducing Resistance/Building Resilience

This is not an easy journey. Constant searching and working to make things happen in your life may make you road weary. In fact, it may be that the reason you are reading this book is that you are simply out of gas. Sometimes, things go wrong. At those times, we tend to try harder, exert more effort toward our goal. But in fact, pushing harder increases resistance. At those times, rather than continue to push, we need to learn to allow and release the obstacles within that are blocking us. Watching your physical and emotional health as guides to the state of your spirit is very important. Pain, illness, and distress of any kind are a signal that something is spiritually wrong—that you are depleted or blocked in some way. As Abraham (*Law of Attraction*), *A Course in Miracles,* and many other sources note, your best indication of whether you are vibrating in alignment with your source is how you feel. So energetic healing, times of peace and regeneration, and the many means of bodywork and stress relief are essential to rebuilding and sustaining your energy, in addition to movement, exercise, and good nutrition.

5. Creating a Plan

Your vision is just the beginning. If you create a clear and compelling vision that describes the spiritual life you want, you can develop a plan to get there by manifesting your desires into the world. That plan involves choosing behaviors that affirm and manifest what you *do* want and continuously build your skills and capabilities to get more of it. Since, as John Lennon said, "Life is what happens when you're making other plans," you can then prepare to be surprised and delighted at what emerges and continue learning from experience. Following each of these five steps will help you to reaffirm or rediscover your purpose, prepare you to take positive action, and set your feet firmly back onto the path of your choosing.

Before you can get to where you're going, though, you must first assess where you are. This is where spiritual autonomy comes in, because that assessment can only be done by you.

Chapter Two

YOUR SPIRITUAL AUTONOMY

*Nothing outside yourself can save you; nothing
outside yourself can bring you peace.*
—*A Course in Miracles*

REDISCOVERING YOUR SACRED PATH means becoming
empowered to independently gather and apply your own
spiritual information and consult your own inner wisdom,
intuition, and feelings regarding whether something is right
for you, rather than taking the word of an ordained "authority" figure (including me) at face value.

I think of autonomy on the spiritual path as being free
to choose and practice the pathway that provides you with
a personal connection to Deity. Once found, applying it in
your daily life involves the conscious, creative use of yourself,
in service to others, toward a purpose worthy of who you are.
You need to be clear about what you stand for, to define the
vision for how you want to be in this world and recognize
that being leads to doing and that the doing is to be of service

in some way. If you do those things well, there will be an exchange of energy that uplifts you and those around you.

With this in mind, you can use the exercises in part 2 of this book to find your own connection to Deity (and to find the path you will ultimately choose to follow) and also to create a plan to demonstrate that connection in action through your work, community, and relationships.

There is now a bewildering assortment of facts, feelings, opinions, and interpretations of "old" religions, shamanic traditions, and new combinations of teachings and disciplines as interest in spirituality has exploded in recent years. But the tools and techniques are not as important as the learning you'll gain in using them. That experience can be strengthened, and your learning accelerated, with some foundational information that may reduce the stress and fear of failure that accompanies doing anything new. I will share tools I have found that help, but there are so many available that this will only serve as a starting point for you to find your own. Because, as we will discuss shortly, you should take no one's word for anything except the opening of new possibilities. If something works for you, keep it. If not, move on.

True Spirituality Is Personal and Experiential

Throughout life, you have been having experiences. Those experiences, from which you have been learning how to be, are why you are here. Right now, you trust your experience over others' words in your life in many ways. Why not in choosing and walking your spiritual path?

We've been living our lives facing outward, and now we need to turn inward and begin asking ourselves questions—become curious about how all these things in our lives got here, whether they still make sense, and what life is really for. We see and feel conditions in our lives that demand change, and instead of doing the same thing over and over again, we seek a new solution.

You are not alone. Many of the people you meet and interact with are in the same situation; you just can't see it in them, because your own inner conflict keeps you focused internally. You haven't failed. You made the best choices you could with the knowledge and experience you had at the time. In this world, nothing stays unchanged forever. For many, it is a spiritual crisis, for others, it is a pragmatic, "real-world" crisis. In both cases, the questions to be answered are the same:

- Where am I going?

- What do I value and believe; what principles will guide me?

- How can I build the capability to focus my intent, knowledge, and skills to make things happen?

- How can I learn what I need to know to sustain me so I don't burn out and give up?

- What do I do next?

These are the questions because what happens is a choice, our choices are based on how we perceive the world, how we perceive is determined by what we think, and what we think is based on what we believe.

Core Values

Autonomy and freedom are two core values shared by most true spiritual paths. Autonomy means you are in control—you decide how, or even whether, to follow a spiritual path and in what way you will do so. Freedom means you can make those choices without fear of Divine judgment or the judgment and control of other people. The very thoughts, feelings, and actions that will lead to fulfillment on a spiritual path violate the behavioral and social requirements of earthly institutions that tell us we are flawed, and we must continually beseech God for forgiveness and to hold back his wrath.

But the Divine is interested in only one thing—that we grow toward reunion with our Source and have experiences that broaden our perspective and increase the wisdom of our Souls. I believe there is one rule, which is ascribed to Wicca but appears in many other philosophies and teachings:

Harm none, including yourself. Beyond that, do what you will.

I consider this rule essential, because the two things that can derail you completely from your path and purpose are guilt and fear. If you appear to harm another, you will experience guilt whether you acknowledge it or bury it, where it will resurface as anger, projected outward. You may also fear retribution. Neither is conducive to the peace, joy, and fulfillment we seek from a spiritual path.

The Cost of Dependence

Few things are as unsettling to someone who has been trained under a tightly controlling system (work, family, church, government) than the phrase "do as you will," because if things go wrong, you have only yourself to blame. You made a choice, as opposed to following the instructions of the perceived authority, and you reap the upside and the downside.

Fear of making a mistake pervades so many belief systems, which creates the need for an intermediary to negotiate forgiveness from God for "sin" that, as some believe, was committed by someone else before you were even here.

There is an important distinction between what we generally speak of as "religion" and a spiritual path or practice. In my view, a religion has a book of scripture, an organization with a clergy structure, a code of conduct, and behavioral expectations that have to do with living this life in a manner considered appropriate. A spiritual path may have some of these but not all. The principle difference is that all spiritual paths are experiential. The intention is to have a direct, autonomous relationship with Spirit. There are teachings, methods, and practices that lead you there, but you choose the method, the path, and the speed at which you travel. On the dogmatic path, you are in trouble with God for failing to abide by the churchly code of conduct. On the spiritual path, you have done nothing wrong in the eyes of the Creator. You may make mistakes and feel you need to make amends in this world to absolve your own guilt, but Deity is not interested in anything other than that you learn the lesson, which always involves forgiveness, and that you be happy. There is no specific time frame to do this work, but forgiveness will always bring peace.

The spiritual paths are experiential. The forms, tools, rituals, techniques, and organizations are many and varied, and can be learned. That is not the hard part. If you have grown up in a dogmatic system and now find yourself embarking on a spiritual path, your first task is to change the way you think and see, from dependence on someone else to make decisions for you to independence, and from accepting others' authority to experiencing your own sovereignty. Then, it's a matter of doing—study and practice. And the guiding principle will be: If it works for you, keep doing it. If it doesn't, move on and try something else.

Growing up in such a dogmatic system is not all bad—you develop a relationship with the Divine, you learn and grow. It is not a "mistake" you need to correct, and the last thing you need is fear of getting it "wrong" again. Han-Shan, the ancient Chinese poet said, "No path goes all the way." You have not made a mistake. The time has simply come to set out on your own, in a new direction.

Different spiritual traditions have different ways of doing things, and if you join them, you agree to honor those ways. However, "honor" does not mean "obey." It's a question of personal integrity—if you make an agreement, you keep it. That does not reduce your freedom—you have made a choice, and you can always choose again. Your key relationship is with Deity—earthly relationships will come, evolve, and perhaps go. You remain in charge of your own destiny.

Once you step on this path, you're on it. No going back. You may pause, you may loiter, but Spirit knows you now, knows you are sincere, wants to help, and couldn't care less about time or space. You have probably been on this road for a while. Your current feeling of being confused, conflicted, or stuck is simply a sign you are reaching a new level of growth, like a snake about to shed the skin it has been wearing for a while in order to accommodate its future size and shape. But the snake won't shed its skin lying still. In order to grow, you need to be in motion.

If you ride a bicycle or motorcycle, you know that speed stabilizes the bike. Standing still, a two-wheeled vehicle between your legs is pretty tippy. But at even a few miles per hour, everything achieves balance, and, at higher speeds, you have rock-solid stability and power to help you deal with all the twists and turns.

Spirit can't help steer you if you're not growing toward your purpose. You're too tippy. And like learning to ride that bike, the lessons in balance can be pretty alarming. But there is also opportunity for tremendous joy, serenity, and fulfillment on the road ahead.

Chapter Three

THE COURAGE TO CHANGE

The essence of independence has been to think and act according to standards from within, not without.

Inevitably anyone with an independent mind must become "one who resists or opposes authority or established conventions": a rebel.

If enough people come to agree with, and follow, the Rebel, we now have a Devil.

Until, of course, still more people agree. And then, finally, we have—Greatness.

—Aleister Crowley

IF YOU ARE READY to step off the edge of your cliff into something new, you are both moving toward something—traveling toward greatness—and, inevitably, leaving some things behind. And some of the people in your life won't like it. You will be seen as a rebel, then a devil, causing problems by not being who you were. But if you stick with it, you will achieve your form of greatness, as Mr. Crowley suggests. Greatness in this case means the most authentic, effective, connected version of who you truly are and expressing the best of who you are in service and action.

The safety and security of the old ways of being will have to be released as you continue your journey. And the experiences you have will change you. It's going to happen anyway, so let's accelerate it.

Grieving for the Old Mode of Being

Your Higher Self is not the only voice claiming your mind's attention. We have each spent many years constructing a persona that is a combination of what we have been taught to be and what we have chosen to be, in order to meet the expectations of our culture and the important people in our lives.

This is our single, most powerful spell—a Thought Form that protects itself and what it has acquired—the ego. The ego we have each created is immediately present and works to maintain its sovereignty through all kinds of resistance to transcending it. Our most powerful addiction may be the ego's need to protect itself.

The first step in the journey is not a stride in a new direction. It is letting go of the safety of the cliff, releasing what no longer serves. Living a life of satisfying others' expectations creates an energetic debt that can manifest as illness, depression, or a sense of alienation because while you are following another's path, the journey to your own purpose is not straight or true. Your Soul will use every experience you have for positive growth, and if you follow your own path instead of that set by others, you can spend less time revisiting old lessons that have yet to be learned.

Letting go of a life in which you have invested significant effort, study, expense, and years or decades just hurts. You may feel grief at losing things or people you value, angry at the loss of years and chances, yearning for things that now cannot happen, or profound regret for what you now see as mistakes for which you can never make amends.

Like losing a loved one, letting go of a life that isn't working can evoke all of the stages of grief identified by Elisabeth Kübler-Ross, as defined below. You may not experience these stages in this sequence and you may alternate among them over a period of time, but it is likely that you will experience all these stages when grieving for your old life.

Shock

Dr. Kübler-Ross wrote of this moment as the reaction to a sudden loss that precedes grief, which changes everything. The sudden awakening that precedes the spiritual search causes you to see yourself and others in a new way. This is the recognition that you have been following a path that has run out, perhaps feeling like you have been spending a great deal of time going in the wrong direction. It may not have been wrong, but it is no longer right, and you can't go back. Your life is out of balance, and you don't know what to do next.

Anger

Whether you discover you have been making life choices to meet others' needs to the exclusion of your own needs or you see you have gradually been making trade-offs that violate your true values, the awareness of an energetic imbalance often manifests as anger and a sense of betrayal. That initial surge of resentment toward those who "used" you to serve their own purposes can be followed by anger toward yourself for choosing to allow it. Ultimately, we have to take responsibility and admit it was a choice. But that can be difficult in this early stage of dealing with change.

Denial

Sometimes the shock is too much, and the anger has no outlet, so we think we must be deluding ourselves and we doubt that it is time to try something new. In my own case, I decided my awakening was not real. After all, everyone else thought all was well. To outward appearances, I had a great life. My sense that something was missing was growing, and seeing no other direction, I changed jobs and cities and started over on the same kind of path that had just run out. It is true that the energy and thought required to start over like that seem like progress. But if it's actually denial, you will know in short order because you will move sideways, not forward.

Spirit often will try to help at this time by offering information in the form of coincidences, omens, and direct events that should give us a clue. I also experienced the gift of a major spiritual insight, which I chose to ignore. It was from this lesson that I learned that nothing is a coincidence.

I lived in New Jersey at the time and was on the cusp of the job change and a new relationship. I decided to drive up to Stokes State Forest, to a section of the Appalachian Trail, and hike until I received some insight.

About thirty minutes into my hike, I sensed a presence behind me—enormous, powerful, and intent. I turned and saw nothing with my physical eyes, but as I paused, I recognized I was at a spot where I had been before—towering rhododendrons flowered all around me, and I knew that through *those two bushes right there* was a rock outcropping overlooking a beautiful valley.

I parted the bushes, dropped my pack, and sat. In a few minutes, a red-tailed hawk flew from right to left at eye level so close I could see the pupil of her left eye.

It is enough to know that the hawk's energy concerns air, intelligence, thinking things through, and considering the short- and long-term vision of your actions, and so combined with the warning of the presence behind me, which, on reflection, represented grounded earth energy, the lesson being relayed was clear: Find my own stability, and use my intelligence, vision, and foresight to decide what was best for me before committing my life to a new direction.

I got enough "data" from that two-hour walk to inform me that I needed to work through my pending divorce, live with my job until then, find my center, and define my autonomous, authentic life path.

But I didn't listen.

Bargaining

I told myself dramatic change wasn't necessary, that I had it figured out. I could put all my energy into work and other people, and become enlightened. This is a prime example of bargaining—books don't read themselves, and there is a reason it is called a spiritual *practice*. I believed that if I gave a little from here or there, if I took a few steps back, or a couple sideways, that I would circumnavigate all my troubles and wind up happy and successful in ways that I had not yet experienced.

I chose not to remember that for Siddhartha (Gautama Buddha) to achieve enlightenment, he had to leave the glitter behind. I reasoned that I was no Buddha, and so maybe I could become a little enlightened and keep on living the "good life." I thought I could bring the spiritual principles I was learning into the workplace, to the organizations that needed it. But they are run by very different rules. I thought I could stay clear in my values and beliefs while serving a very different kind of vision. Truth is, you become what you do.

Depression

The strategy of trying to outrun my own intuition finally failed. And knowing no other way to proceed, I found myself in despair.

Nothing worked. If I was functioning, I was only going through the motions. Like the Kansas scenes in *The Wizard of Oz,* my world had gone to shades of grey. I kept trying half-measures—occasionally using the tools of spirituality that were at my fingertips, and yet the outcome was always the same.

Nothing worked. Or, more accurately, everything worked to the degree I was investing energy and intention into it, which was—not much. Actually, any of the disciplines I tried could have healed me, gotten me moving, if I had only used them consistently. But that is the nature of depression—sustained effort is nearly impossible.

So there I was caught in the effects of the economic downturn of 2008, and I was living the life I had designed but that was completely different from my Soul calling, and I had no way out. So it was time to accept my fate, live the lifestyle until my big heart attack took me out, and let everyone talk about what a great guy I had been. In the process of giving up, I didn't realize I was finally letting go so the Universe could take over.

Hope

Now, up to this point, I had decided I was done with spirituality—I had two traditional religions and multiple New Age practices under my belt, so I figured I knew what was available.

Until I arrived at a used book sale. It was there that I found *Wicca and Witchcraft for the Complete Idiot*. I figured, "why not? I certainly qualify" and bought the book. Then I thought, what if I really apply this and see if it works?

And I discovered two things—I believed it, and it did. As I reflected on why I was doing it, I realized I had dabbled in those other things—learned them but not practiced them with discipline. I asked myself if I was ready to try going deep this time, and really dig in. I decided to try and, in trying, soon realized I had stood up and was beginning to move forward on my path again.

I began to realize that I was forging a new path in the right direction and that this experiential path had emotion, intensity, challenge, and—heart. And my ups became longer while my downs became more shallow. And I began to believe that perhaps there was a way to recover my commitment and ability to take this journey, and it was going to be different, but that was OK. I had found hope, the sustainable energy to move forward on my path.

Acceptance

Now, this is the last stage, but it is not the end. It is the beginning—the moment when, in perfect love and perfect trust, one prepares to step off that cliff again into the unknown.

And in so doing, you discover all the things you have to clean up to really make progress. It is not enough to exert effort in your chosen direction; you also have to remove the obstacles that you have placed in the way of your own growth. Some refer to this as doing your "shadow" work—identifying those internal energetic and psychological blocks to growth that must be resolved. In my own case, I finally understood that my problem was not external situations or other people. The life situations that were causing my unhappiness were the result of my responses and my choices. And when I began to make other choices, situations began to change.

I committed myself to both Wicca and the healing energy of Reiki. And with those disciplines, I have found that I have returned to my own path, and it incorporates the lessons of everything I have done in the past. And I can continue on this path knowing that lessons and difficulties will be there to face, learning must go on forever, and there will be times I am discouraged and feel like giving up. But now I know how to recover.

There are no shortcuts through these stages of grieving for your former path and former life. In fact, I wouldn't want to give them to you even if I could. My hope is that by exploring and acknowledging these stages of grief, that you will see each seeming switchback and detour as part of your Soul's process in this life, and embrace the lesson.

Some Thoughts on Resistance

Before you can focus and direct energy toward conscious, helpful action, you have to become a clear channel for that energy. That involves a lot of inner work. And inner work is not easy. We resist it and distract ourselves from it. You can acquire intellectual knowledge, tools, techniques, and practice rituals and spells or your chosen method of manifestation, but if you find things are not manifesting, or you are manifesting the opposite of what your words request, you are out of alignment with your Higher Self. In other words, your ego is resisting the call of Spirit.

It can be a challenge to let go of the certainty of the intellect. As children, we learn in an almost completely experiential way. Before we have language, we use taste, smell, hearing, touch, sight to learn about our world. We also very quickly develop intuition. We learn who the safe people are, and then, as we meet strangers, we have one of three reactions—indifference, joy, or fear. And then there is the matter of invisible friends, talking trees, the sound of color, and the color of sound—all part of childhood perception when we are close to Spirit on that end of life.

Then we go to school, and our developing frontal lobe is taught to override the natural flow of information from Spirit. We are taught the rules and the content of a rational life.

And it works—because the entire system of which we are a part has been built to reinforce it. This is not entirely bad. We need this knowledge and skill to fulfill our purpose here.

The problem is that we end up excluding the other forms of perception along the way.

Gordon Mackenzie, who worked for a major greeting card company, used to speak in schools about creativity. He would ask second graders, "How many of you are artists?" Almost every hand went up. In high school, a few hands would go up. Somewhere in between, art, creativity, intuition, and the simple joy of Spirit became unimportant, even unreal.

That art is separated from science makes sense to us—and we learn to use science for decision making. If every time we do X, Y occurs, we come to expect Y. When Z occurs, we either don't perceive it or we become angry or fearful.

But—things that can't possibly happen, do. A frail woman lifts a car off of her injured child. Cancer mysteriously goes into remission. A psychic intuitive locates a missing child. You start a sentence to your significant other, "When our son calls—" interrupted by the ringing phone.

As we gain experience and perspective, we notice that there is a tenuous correlation between church membership and the quality of compassion a person exhibits. There can be an inverse relationship between academic success and success in the "real world." Those who think "outside the box" are the makers of breakthroughs and insights. Those who think inside the box count the results of innovation. And we realize—or remember?—there is "something else."

Which brings us to the question of belief. If something is determined to be true using the scientific method, we tend to overlook those times when it turns out not to work quite that way.

In September 2012, European physicists clocked some neutrinos travelling just a bit faster than light. The experts said if those results were replicated, it would threaten the foundation of physics and modern science.

In June 2013, the experiment was repeated, and the neutrinos reached light speed but did not exceed it. It is interesting to note that the intention of the first researcher was to make neutrinos exceed the speed of light, and the intention of the second was to prove that they couldn't.

Measurement aside, the second scientist seems to have disregarded Werner Heisenberg (The Uncertainty Principle), Massimiliano Sassoli de Bianchi (The Observer Effect), and others who have created a body of logic that indicates the presence of the observer in an experiment, particularly with subatomic particles, affects the outcome of the experiment. There is no such thing as a passive observer. Thoughts are things, and they influence the environment.

So the logical case can easily be made that neutrinos are very obliging creatures—the original research team desperately wanted to achieve greater-than-light speeds, and they did. And the follow-up researchers desperately wanted to preserve the status quo, and they did.

However, no matter how many stories, articles, and books are written about psychics accurately finding lost people, or hands-on healing methods reversing the course of illness, our culture thinks of these things as "woo woo" and they are dismissed. Our culture discounts the successes of approaches it considers "alternative."

Resistance is something that is engrained in us from childhood and reinforced by all of the experiences we have while we grow. The problem with this is that resistance can severely limit our awareness, our perceptions, and even our options, especially when it comes to treading a new path—or one that is not conventionally accepted. To embark on your new path, there are things you will need to learn and unlearn. The key is to be aware of your resistance and begin to unravel it so that you can clear the path to your true purpose.

Resolving Resistance

See if you can complete this sentence before reading farther:
I would like to learn and practice _____
[Druidism, Chinese Medicine, Wicca, Magic, Energy Healing, Buddhism . . .] regularly, but—

Choose one of the below:

Others' judgment

- My non-Pagan friends will think I'm weird

- My friends and family know about this stuff but see it as a party game and they'll make fun of me for taking it seriously

Logistical issues

- I don't have time

- I have no privacy

- Tools and resources are not available to me

Uncertainty and doubt

- I might do things wrong—and it won't work

- I might misinterpret the Tarot cards or Runes, miss the point, and get it all wrong

- I may inadvertently offend the Oracle if I don't do this right

- I might do a reading for someone else and it won't make sense to them

Some Guiding Principles

Let there be beauty and strength,
power and compassion, honor and humility,
mirth and reverence within you . . .
—The Charge of the Goddess

This phrase in *The Charge of the Goddess* elegantly describes the mental and spiritual state required to walk in beauty on the spiritual path. I make no claim that I have mastered any one of these tools or am somehow enlightened. I have made my share of mistakes—notably, I once left my Tarot cards out to be charged by the full moon in reach of a sprinkler system that comes on during the night—and I'm sure I will make more.

But I hope my reverence and respect for these tools and their history come through. I find mirth and reverence to be a very necessary combination.

A mentor once said to me that the best leaders and teachers help you see the way they see, rather than telling you what to do. There are multiple learning styles—some of us need to start with the big picture and then delve into the details.

Some need to see the pieces and how they fit together in order to understand the full puzzle. But ultimately, we all need the whole picture.

As I discussed earlier, there are certain aspects of Paganism that run throughout all traditions and branches. The three principles below are what I have found to be common in Pagan spiritualties.

The Rede

Known as the Wiccan Rede, this principle appears in some way in most spiritual paths I know of:

"An it harm none, do as ye will."

We touched briefly on this principle previously, and it can be a great boon in helping you discover the path that is meant for you, rather than following someone else's.

Though it sounds simple in principle, this is not always so easy to do. "Harm" can be a subjective thing (anything from physical harm to hurting someone's feelings) and remember, "none" includes yourself.

While it can be difficult to try to follow this principle to the letter in every single action, it is best to strive for it at least in your intent. If you approach a task with the intention of doing no harm to, or even helping, yourself or others, you will do well.

The Law of Three

Everything we do, positive or hurtful, returns to us as many times as required for us to learn the lesson. Divination readings or some form of focusing and directing energy for self or others, done with helpful intent, will return helpfulness. This assumes you have done the work of learning how to use the thought systems involved. It doesn't mean every reading will predict good fortune or every spell or ritual will produce a successful outcome. It does mean you should accept the results you get, interpret them honestly and authentically, tell the truth, and choose how to use them in your life with integrity.

The Pyramid

You must understand—know—the principles, tools, and techniques you are using; develop the ability and generate the energy—the will—to do what you are about to do; dare to follow through on it by taking action in the physical world to manifest your desired result; and keep your own counsel.

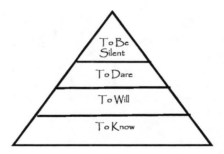

"Being silent" is not a question of hiding or shame. You are best served by not subjecting yourself or your practice to verbal abuse or ridicule. No one needs to know what you're doing, and when you are new to something, the surest way to kill your motivation is to have someone throw cold water on the idea.

Once you have developed some confidence, and you have some successful readings and manifestations behind you, you will have the assurance to tell people that it's something you find helpful and leave it at that. No one has to approve.

The autonomous seeker does not need permission.

Do What You Will (But Don't Mess Up)

Most books on spiritual practices teach the history, cosmology, and spiritual significance of the system in question, then delve into the symbols, rituals, and practices required to gain the desired answer or knowledge. Emphasis is often placed on doing everything exactly right or you may not get the desired result, and, in some cases, you may offend the Higher Spirit behind the situation.

No pressure.

As a novice, over and over I sat and looked at the wrapped box of Tarot cards and the branch I had cut for the Runes I wanted to make, and each time I just knew I was going to mess up somehow.

If you are a beginner at something, you will inevitably do it better tomorrow than you will today. After many years of spiritual work and study, I came to the conclusion that I wasn't in this to feel guilty, and a little joy might even be in order. So I developed these ideas, which guide the remainder of this work.

Intention is everything

It is necessary to approach divination, spell work, path working, journeying, and magic with a clear intent and respect for Spirit. If your heart and mind clearly hold the singular thing you need or the question you need answered, Spirit will help. For example, in Usui Reiki, it is believed that if you begin a treatment with the intent to heal, and draw the healing symbols incorrectly, Spirit will correct them for you. Similarly, Spirit knows what is truly in your heart as you cast the Runes or draw your cards, or anoint and burn your candle, and will answer your true question. So if the reading makes no sense, examine your mind-set and clarity of your intent.

That said, it is important to be focused and clear

While there is not a spiritual sergeant at arms waiting to cleave you in two if you miss a word or two in your ritual preparation, it is critically important to ask one, unambiguous question when consulting a divination tool and have one singular intention when doing spell work or other forms of manifestation. Otherwise, you can't be sure what the message is, or which aspect of your multipart inquiry is being addressed. In spell work, focusing on what you don't want may bring exactly that into manifestation. A scattered mind will yield scattered information and ambiguous results. As Abraham and other teachers have told us repeatedly, you manifest what you focus on.

Spirit does not care about time

Time and space are constructs of this world. Last year, I kept doing three-card readings on the same question every couple of weeks and getting the same answer. Finally, I got the distinct message to quit asking—Spirit seemed to be saying, "We get it. We know what you want. Now pay attention and listen. It will appear when conditions are right." And as things have unfolded, I have experienced the coming together of "external" conditions in some cases, and in others, the realization that I needed to change to come into alignment with what I was trying to manifest.

Spirit has a sense of humor

Many experienced shamans and elders in any tradition are jokesters. We must remember that we are here to create and experience joy. This is not a schoolroom where our knuckles are rapped by the teacher for getting the answer wrong. If we were perfect, we would not be here. We do get to experience the consequences of our actions, but that is a different matter, and it is not "punishment."

While smiles and laughter are likely, it is important to remember we are dealing with archetypal forces, and there is a difference between an honest slip and simply not taking things seriously. I've experienced Ouija board sessions leading to terrifying messages because they were used as party games or approached in a flippant manner.

It is best to avoid using any oracle, or attempting to direct energy toward a desired outcome, when under the influence of alcohol or drugs. It is not respectful, and practically speaking, you will have a harder time maintaining focus and clear intention.

So we have asked what brings us here, and I've shared some of my experiences, changes, and disappointments, which may have allowed you to reflect on your own.

We have addressed how we learn, from a process and a psychological perspective. We have talked about the resistance that can be born from fear when you embark on this path. And we've introduced the idea of using divination and manifestation tools and techniques to gather your own spiritual information and focus your intention on making things happen.

I end this section with perhaps the most encouraging and reassuring spiritual principle I have ever found—the frame of reference underpinning *A Course in Miracles*:

Nothing real can be threatened.
Nothing unreal exists.
Therein lies the Peace of God.

Chapter Four

THE POWER AND HEALING FRAMEWORK FOR LEARNING AND GROWTH

A path is only a path, and there is no affront, to oneself or to others, in dropping it if that is what your heart tells you. Look at every path closely and deliberately. Try it as many times as you think necessary. Then ask yourself alone, one question: Does this path have a heart? If it does, the path is good; if it doesn't it is of no use.

—Carlos Castaneda, *The Teachings of Don Juan*

ALL OF THE PHILOSOPHIZING and thinking in the world will not change your life if you don't do something about the insights you have gained. Just this morning, as I sat down to meditate and ask my Spirit Guides for helpful information, I felt compelled to go over the last few weeks of entries to look for guidance I had not yet put into practice. Those leftovers can become an energetic drain. Procrastination hurts.

So taking the first step towards changing your spiritual practice is crucial because unless you do it while your resolve is still fresh, you will lose your nerve, the book will go on the shelf, and you will delay your progress.

It begins with passion. Passion is the surge of energy and motivation that arises when you are attracted to something new. It is, literally, falling in love with that thing. But passion can only take you so far—it's like the starter motor in your car. Its purpose is not to move the car forward, but rather to engage the larger engine, where the real power is. Your passion for your newfound path—the love you feel for it—provides enthusiasm. We will address passion by asking you to reflect on what brings you here. Why are you having this conversation with yourself? What conditions in your life must be released or brought into being? Knowing your starting point is essential to building the map to your destination.

Before we define your destination, consider what values and principles are most important. What will guide you? These may include the Rede—do no harm—or characteristics and attributes like integrity, honesty, direct and clear communication. They may also include others—values such as family, community, or service to others in some specific or general way. These are the guardrails for your next spiritual journey. Your choice of tools, actions, and approaches will be guided by these principles.

Once you know your starting point and the rules by which you will travel, it is time to formulate a clear and compelling vision for what your life will be like when you are up and running on your new spiritual path.

Then, having defined your destination and your starting point, you will consider your capacity—the capabilities you need to realize your vision. Some of these may be strengths

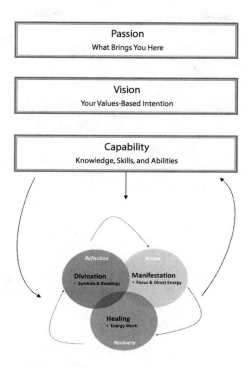

you already possess; some may be knowledge, skills, or attributes you need to acquire. Since we are talking about a spiritual path here, our focus will be on capabilities for:

Divination—Gathering intuitive and spiritual information from within your own being and from spirit guides and others on the many planes of existence

Manifestation—Focusing and directing energy toward a desired outcome

Healing—Recovering from the setbacks, bumps, and bruises that accompany doing anything important or new

You will then get on with it—working the cycle of reflection, manifestation, and recovery to enable your Soul's growth in the direction of reunion with Deity.

Because this is deep inner work, it is necessary that you build skills of clearing excess and unfocused energy, centering, grounding, and shielding yourself from distracting energies. You will become more sensitive to the emotional and energetic climate around you, and so it is important that you be able to maintain your balance.

In the second half of this book, I will share techniques for developing and refining your vision using divination, manifestation, and healing as the basis for developing your new plan, but, for now, I would like you to focus on the basic techniques of centering yourself. This will be the first step to performing any of the advanced techniques.

Chapter Five

CENTERING FOR POWER
AND HEALING

Realize deeply that the present moment is all you have.
Make the NOW the primary focus of your life.
—Eckhard Tolle

YOU WILL BE USING energy in some form in every activity we will undertake together. You use energy all the time, every day, to get things done. In many cases, that energy isn't focused and directed with full intention, and if it is, we move on from one period of intensity to another, often without taking the time to clear our minds and move our bodies to get ready for a fresh start on the next task. We are often driven by the urgent rather than the important, by the immediate rather than the long-term.

The process we will use in this book will require you to intensely focus and direct your energy in three very specific ways:

- Visualizing and setting intention for your
  spiritual path;

- Gathering spiritual information from your Higher Self, your Spirit Guides, and other sources; and

- Acting to manifest your vision by:

  - Affirming your intention on a regular basis through tools like spell work and ritual;

  - Taking action in the world of form.

Because each of these requires a great deal of focused concentration and you will be raising energy every time, it is extremely important that you be centered when you start and that you clear excess energy and release it to the Universe so it can be recycled for the good of all and not hang around you, getting in the way of your focus and intent.

Allowing unfocused energy to remain within your own energy field or aura can cause blockages that can manifest as feelings of being spacey, fatigued, and overwhelmed, so it is important to clear and release. You must center before beginning any visualization, divination, or manifestation activity and then clear and release the excess energy when you have released the intention to the Universe.

These are good habits to get into even in your daily activities (before and after meetings or when starting and finishing work on a project). In fact, doing so will deepen and strengthen your skills for your spiritual work as well.

Clearing and Releasing

Clearing your energy is the process by which you let go of any energies that are not serving you or that you do not wish to hold onto. These could be stresses related to work (like the phrase "taking your work home with you"), health, family, etc. It is important to clear your energy to make sure that you are holding onto only the positive energies that you want to keep, instead of keeping unconscious attachments to old or detrimental energies.

"Clearing" your energy happens in two phases—first, assessing your current physical and mental state for any tension, anxiety, worry, or pain and becoming clear on what has to stay and what has to go. Feelings of comfort, peace, and well-being can stay. Tension, anxiety, and pain can go.

"Releasing" is the process by which you let go of the old energies that you wish to be rid of. Releasing involves allowing yourself to be fully aware of the "negative" (really, unfocused) energy and using your exhaled breath to let go of those energies and allow the affected part of your body or mind to relax. The exercise below is an example of how to do this. Perform the exercise for a minimum of five minutes, a maximum of ten; whatever is comfortable for you.

Close your eyes and visualize that you are being gently cleansed by water.

If you are lying down, imagine you are lying on a warm, smooth rock in a warm and gentle river and feel the water flowing by you. Imagine the water level rises to just below your ears.

If you are seated, imagine a waterfall above your head gently cascading warm, soft water that flows down your body and into the earth.

Take several slow, deep breaths, inhaling slowly to a count of three, pausing briefly, then exhaling slowly to a count of three and pausing again.

As you do so, quiet your mind and think only of your breathing. If a thought enters your mind, notice it and let it flow through into the water to be carried away to be dealt with later.

Return to your normal pattern of breathing and mentally scan your body from your head to your toes, noticing every body part, and allowing it to relax into the surface that supports you, whether you are lying down or sitting up.

If you notice any sign of tension, pain, or discomfort, take a deep breath as above and intensify your awareness of the feeling during the inhale, and release the feeling into the meditative water that surrounds you by pushing it out through the bottoms of your feet as you exhale.

Continue your body scan as above, working through each area of pain or tension as you discover them.

When your body scan is complete, relax even further and be aware of the water carrying away all tension, unfocused energy, and stress.

Remain in this state until you feel no sign of blockage, tension, or stress and your body is warm, heavy, and relaxed.

Open your eyes.

Practice this exercise at the beginning of your day and before going to sleep at night. You may find it helps you get to sleep and stay asleep more easily, as you have dispelled all the "leftovers" of your day.

We will recall this exercise at each stage of the process and note when and how to use it.

Major chakras

The chakras are the seven major energy vortices within your etheric body. The chakra system is a network like your circulatory system that distributes energy through your etheric or astral body and energizes your physical body. If you are unfamiliar with chakras, a diagram appears below. The next meditation we will discuss is designed to orient you to them and their purposes, and introduce you to how they support you energetically.

Imbalances or blockages in this energy system are often the cause of distress or lack of well-being in the areas each chakra governs. The chakra system is the basis for acupuncture, acupressure, and the many forms of energy healing.

There are thousands of chakra points in the body. These are the major ones, the energy centers that receive, distribute, and give energy and govern major physical, emotional, and spiritual processes.

Basic Grounding and Centering

Most of us live in our heads—we are constantly thinking, reading, evaluating, assessing, conceptualizing about our work, our world, and making rational plans to deal with what we discover.

5–THROAT CHAKRA: Light Blue

- Speech, sound, vibration, communication
- Creative expression in speech, writing, the arts
- Integration, peace, truth, wisdom, knowledge, loyalty
- Turquoise, chrysocolla, celestite, blue topaz, other light blue stones

7–CROWN CHAKRA: Violet

- Top of Head
- Governs thought, Connection to Higher Self
- Vitalizes upper brain
- Spiritual will, inspiration, perception beyond space and time
- Amethyst, Diamond, Sugilite, Selenite

4–HEART CHAKRA: Green

- Center of chest
- Anchors life force from higher self
- Energizes life force for body's systems
- Divine/unconditional love, forgiveness, compassion, balance, acceptance
- Emerald, malachite, rose quartz, ruby

6–BROW (Third Eye) CHAKRA: Indigo/Purple

- Center of forehead, between the eyebrows
- Vitalizes lower brain, CNS, vision
- Spiritual insight and perception
- Intuition, insight, imagination, clairvoyance, peace of mind, perception beyond the material
- Lapis Lazuli, Azurite, Sodalite, quartz, sapphire, blue tourmaline

3–SOLAR PLEXUS CHAKRA: Yellow

- Abdomen to behind the navel
- Vitality to sympathetic nervous system, metabolism, adrenals
- Will, personal power, energy, authority, self control, humor, joy
- Citrine, amber, gold topaz, tiger eye, gold

2–NAVEL CHAKRA: Orange

- Lower abdomen to navel
- Procreation, sexuality, physical force and vitality
- Giving and receiving, emotions, desire, sexuality/passion, change, movement, family
- Carnelian, coral, gold calcite, orange stones

1–ROOT CHAKRA: Red/Black

- Base of spine (tailbone)
- Physical vitality–life force, survival, self-preservation, instinct
- Material success and issues, physical body, grounding, individuality, stability, security, courage, patience
- Ruby, garnet, bloodstone, red jasper, obsidian, smoky quartz

Grounding is a method for getting out of your head and into your root chakra, stabilizing your energy in the here and now. Essentially, you are lowering your energetic center of gravity so you are fully present in your body, aware of what you are seeing, hearing, smelling, touching, and feeling emotionally.

Centering is literally coming to the awareness of your center—once grounded and secure in your root chakra—being able to visualize a plumb line from the center of the earth through your body to the limits of the heavens. You are fully present and aligned with all that is.

For this exercise, use the previous clearing and releasing exercise first to deeply relax your body and mind.

Next, imagine a white ball of energy above your head that sends a beam of loving, nurturing, powerful energy into the top of your head, through your seven major chakras, out your feet, and into the earth through energetic roots.

Draw corresponding energy up from the earth as well, and the two beams of loving energy will join in you, where heaven and earth, spirit and matter, become one.

Chakra Balancing Meditation for Grounding and Centering

The previous chart indicates the function of each chakra in regulating our well-being in their respective aspects. If any chakra is depleted, there will be difficulty in the area that chakra governs, as well as effects throughout the system.

So it is important to ensure that your chakras are clear and strong and there is a good flow of energy throughout. The exercise below is one method for balancing your chakras.

Again, begin by using the clearing and releasing method on the previous pages.

When you have achieved your most relaxed state, return to a normal pattern of breathing.

Visualize a ball of brilliant white light and energy above your head, about where your hands would be if you raised them fully over your head with palms together.

Imagine a beam of gentle, powerful energy entering the crown of your head and, as it does so, a ball of brilliant lavender light forming at the top of your head—your crown chakra, which connects you to divine knowledge and insight. This ball begins to spin clockwise, and as it does so, you are aware of your connection to your higher self and have access to your Soul's knowledge.

The beam of light travels down into the center of your head, behind your eyes, where a beautiful deep indigo ball of light forms and begins to spin clockwise. This is your third-eye chakra, and the energy is supporting your intuition and spiritual sight.

When you have visualized your third-eye chakra, imagine the light continues down to your throat area, where a brilliant turquoise ball of light forms, energizing your throat chakra, which empowers you to integrate the knowledge and perception of your upper chakras and speak your truth.

The beam of light continues down to your heart area, where a ball of beautiful emerald green light forms and begins to spin clockwise. Your values, and the ability to give and receive love, are encouraged and nurtured in this center.

The light continues down to your solar plexus, where a ball of brilliant yellow light forms and begins to spin clockwise.

Your solar chakra is the seat of your will and your connection to the Divine.

The light flows down behind your navel, to your sacral chakra. A ball of brilliant orange light begins to spin clockwise behind your navel. Your sacral chakra is the center for creativity, sexuality, and your capacity for joy.

Finally, the light reaches the base of your spine, where a ball of brilliant scarlet light begins to spin clockwise. This is your root chakra, which governs your sense of purpose and place in the world of form.

From your root chakra, imagine energetic roots reaching down into the earth as far as you can take them. Imagine they are wrapping around a stone, a crystal, or a shell and from that source they begin pulling up strong earth energy, which flows up those roots, enters your root chakra, and continues up each chakra, joining and circulating with the energy of the heavens that you pulled down through your crown chakra. In you, spirit and matter are one. And so the energy of the earth and the energy of the heavens empower and strengthen you, grounding you in your identity and purpose.

Visualize the ball of light above your head again and recognize it is your connection to your Higher Self. Ask your Higher Self to inspire you in the work you are about to undertake and to help you gain insight and learning to help you on your path. Listen for a while for words, images, feelings, and impressions that may have something to do with your request. If you are new to this kind of meditation, you may wonder whether it's your "imagination" or a real message from Spirit. The relevance of the impression or message you get to the question you asked is one clue, and the other is to make note of what you perceive and then see how it plays out in action later on.

When you are finished, visualize each chakra closing down and returning to a restful state from your crown to your root, knowing that your energy has been aligned and you are grounded and "on purpose."

Create a journal to note any insights or ideas.

Shielding and Protection

We are energetic beings. Most of us exercise very little control over the way we take in and express that energy. We have the ability to affect others and are susceptible to being affected by the energy of others in turn. As your sensitivity to energy grows, you may find yourself affected by others' energy.

All interactions involve an exchange of energy. If the exchange is not balanced, one party may feel uplifted by the interaction while the other feels depleted. I have experienced this in the training setting. When a group is quiet and not engaged, I find myself putting out more energy to enliven the session. When the group is engaged, there is a mutual exchange of energy that creates a dynamic and enjoyable session.

So when you feel an imbalance of energy, your first order of business is to quickly ground and center to establish your own equilibrium. Then, use a technique like the one below to protect your own energy. Depending on the situation, you can either remove the source of the imbalance, remove your-self from the situation, or change the dynamics of the situation in some way.

The need for such shielding and protection is very heavily influenced by your beliefs. If you believe that someone can cast a spell on you and that such a thing will cause you harm, then it is possible you will experience the effects.

If you find yourself easily influenced by the energy of a group or an individual or an environment, you may benefit from some simple shielding. If this continues to be an issue for you, you may wish to do further study on the subject using the resources noted in the appendix.

To go "shields up," after performing the grounding and centering meditation, visualize your aura—a bubble of beautiful energy surrounding your body to a distance of up to 6 feet in all directions—and mentally place a mirror surrounding your aura. Hold the intention that this mirror is amplifying and protecting your energy and permitting only healing and loving energy to enter and connect with you. Now imagine there is also a mirror on the outside, facing away from you. For this technique, hold the intention that this mirror repels all unfocused or negative energy back to its source. End this brief meditation by repeating, "I allow only positive and loving energies to enter my aura, and I repel all negative or harmful energies. I am safe. I am protected."

Once you are shielded from stray or negative energies, you should find it easier to interact with certain groups, individuals, or environments that may have previously been the cause of stress and tension.

PART TWO

Gaining Insight for Resuming Your Journey by Using Divination, Manifestation, and Healing

Chapter Six

AN INTRODUCTION TO DIVINATION

He opened the book at random, or so he believed, but a book is like a sandy path which keeps the indent of footsteps.
—Graham Greene, *The Human Factor*

DIVINATION INVOLVES THE practice of seeking meaning and guidance from your inner-wisdom Divine and Spiritual sources through the use of omens, events, and systems of symbols that have come to have their own integrity and purpose over time.

This is our first practical departure from conventional dogmatic practice. As Carl Jung has said, "One of the main functions of formalized religions is to protect people against a direct experience of God." Divination and its partner, conscious manifestation, are the two primary means of attaining that direct experience.

Divination relies on symbols arranged in a structure of meaning that allows you to access your inner guidance, bypassing your "left brain" analytical and judging function. Symbols reach us at a very deep psychological level. The symbols we will encounter in the two divination systems we discuss here—the Germanic Runes and the Tarot—seem to be shared at a Soul level. These two systems are Western in origin. There are many, many others among other cultures.

In practice, divination is used to ask a question when faced with a problem or need. In the everyday world, we might consult a therapist, clergy or other counselor, or a wise friend. The best advice we receive is usually when the person in question consults their intuition and, in conversation, helps us go deeper for the answer. Tarot and Runes allow us to do the same thing and consult our own inner sources and Spirit as we relate to it—angels, guides, masters—for the answer.

Chances are that someone who thinks they are new to divination has actually used it. Checking the weather forecast before planning a picnic is seeking guidance about the future. Flipping a coin and saying, "Heads, I buy twenty lottery tickets. Tails, I wait until next week," is using divination. But conventional wisdom is funny about divination.

If you are brand new to divination, I highly recommend you begin by seeking out a skilled Tarot reader and someone adept at Rune readings. Focus on a significant question with meaning for your life before you go to each, and experience the process and the outcome for yourself. Remember my earlier comment about coincidence—do not worry about finding the "right" reader—if you approach a reputable metaphysical bookstore or attend an established psychic fair, you can assume the reader you find was the right one for you at the time.

Why Use Divination?

It can increase confidence and help you avoid possible pitfalls.

When faced with a decision or an upcoming event of some importance, many people will do a Rune or Tarot drawing to get a sense of the influences surrounding the situation. It allows you to be prepared, which can increase confidence that you will know what to do when the time comes and your sense that Spirit has weighed in (or will weigh in) on your behalf. It can also help you avoid influences that may be present in the situation.

Divination can add meaning and richness to life by helping you see and act on the interactions and influences among people, places, things, and events.

A couple of years ago, I was riding my motorcycle from Seattle to the Oregon Coast. Because of heavy traffic, I arrived in Portland to see a beautiful sunset with ninety minutes of travel ahead of me, in the dark, on a two-lane road that wound through forest and over the mountains of the Clatsop State Forest. With traffic coming on my left and pitch black woods full of elk and deer on my right, I felt extremely exposed. I wasn't so worried about the cars—I was much more concerned about an animal choosing to cross the road in front of me, which would have ended my journey, on multiple levels, pretty quickly. I asked and prayed for protection and support, feeling tense and tight and cold.

As I rounded a bend, I saw the beautiful first-quarter moon clear the trees, and suddenly—I was in the Moon card of the Tarot, a card symbolic of navigating our life path while practicing inner work to cut through the haze of illusion. And I took it as a message that if I stayed fully present and was not preoccupied by the illusion of fear, I would have all the tools I needed to make it through the journey. I gave thanks, relaxed (which helped me warm up), and gave the bike a little more gas. I completed the journey safely and actually enjoyed the ride. The moon stayed right over the road in front of me most of the time.

Had I not known about the Moon card, I would have had exactly the same physical experience. But my emotional experience would have been very different. And emotion and thought drive behavior. If I were riding in tension and fear, and an animal did leap out at me, I might have overreacted and had a very bad outcome.

How a System Might Develop

It might have gone this way:

> A young man awakens to the buzz of cicadas. His lodge is already warm, typical for summer in the Everglades. It's an important day—the holy man of his village has declared him ready for his first hunt, and today is the day.
>
> After ritual preparation, the Blessing by the Clan Mothers, and a light breakfast with his father and a group of men, he takes his bow and knife into the pine forest. The sun rises higher, the heat intensifies. He almost loses focus until he hears a rustling in the undergrowth, and a doe startled by his presence stands twenty feet away. He nocks an arrow, aims, and fires. Heart shot.
>
> Back at the village that evening, the celebration feast ended, he can't sleep. Sitting by the fire, he carves an image of the deer from a piece of wood and silently thanks the Great Spirit and the Spirit

of the deer for the gift of game that means food, clothing, and other material for the family.

A few days later, he goes out on his second hunt. The story is repeated with his first wild pig. As the weeks go by, green sea turtles, bear, and other game fall to his bow. Each time, he carves an image to honor the spirit of the animal, which he places in a bag he has made to hold them.

One morning, he awakens and prepares to hunt. He looks at his bag of animal fetishes and wonders what game he will get today. He asks the Great Spirit for guidance—a prediction—and asks that the animal who will provide the gift of sustenance today be made known to him. He pulls the deer, and a deer it is. Soon, other hunters ask to use the bag. A ritual forms around it. Additional rituals are performed to try to ensure success.

His confidence builds, and, one night at dusk, he is walking through the forest and comes eye to eye with a black panther. He reaches for his bow, but lowers his arm. They look at each other for long minutes, and he feels an energetic relationship ignite between two hunters. The panther turns and disappears into the brush. Our young man has learned, by experience, the difference between hunting and killing.

Now, before each hunt, he meditates on becoming one energetically with the spirit of the panther. Then he draws an image from the pouch. He now sees the whole living system from the perspective of

Spirit. And in his dreams, he merges and runs with
the panther.

And so a tool for divination may be born. It contains
three elements:

- A set of symbols with great emotional meaning
  to the individual

- A ritual for accessing the symbols and their
  meaning

- A guiding frame of reference that connects
  symbols, ritual, and the life experience of the
  practitioner into a unified whole

When all elements are aligned, the interpretation of the
symbols provides guidance regarding the likely outcome of
the intention, or the answer to the question, and insight into
the conditions affecting success. Many people would say that
the outcome of the hunt would be the same without the ritual—that it is about the skill of the hunter, not the image
chosen from the bag.

But the ritual and practice surrounding the hunt add
meaning to the process and the outcome. That meaning will
give the hunter confidence and focus. A skilled, confident,
focused person will always outperform a skilled, uncertain,
unfocused person. And Spirit has been alerted to need and
intention. When your feelings, intentions, and energy are
aligned, the universe responds. Personally, I believe that a spiritual connection is created between the hunter and the animal.

What could you accomplish if your spirit guides assured you that you would succeed?

Some say the guidance received from divination is received from Spirit. Some say it is the individual's intuition or subconscious alerting them in a language they can understand that, assuming current course and speed, their destination is inevitable. In conversation after one of my journeys, I expressed to the shamanic counselor my worry that it was "all in my mind." He said, "Now you see how vast your mind really is."

If you are already one with Deity, and one with all things, then all forms of journeying, path working—and divination—can help you gain access to the information, insight, and guidance available from all of those aspects of self and Spirit. So yes, It is All in our minds—and our minds are in the All.

Every culture has developed a system or systems of divination. Success in learning and interpreting the oracles requires an openness to learning, a willingness to be surprised, and the ability to notice what you notice.

Each system of divination has a spiritual and philosophical basis (which I'll call its "cosmology"), a set of rituals and practices associated with its use, and a method (or methods) of interpretation that allows the user to obtain the guidance they are seeking.

Cosmology

All systems of divination can be used without subscribing to a particular belief system. Tarot cards, for example, are used by practicing members of many religions who believe that Deity as they understand Her (or Him) is using that method to communicate with them either directly or through intermediaries such as spirit guides, angels, and the like. There are also those who use these tools as party entertainment, or a thrilling flirtation with "the unknown." But that mind-set yields the results it deserves.

However, accurate interpretation requires that you know the belief system and the meaning of the symbols and their implications. I will be presenting the original and foundational frame of reference for each system so it is clear what forces and energies are in play. Given my likely audience, I doubt there are many flirts among you.

There is a difference of opinion regarding whether casting your own readings is advisable, as opposed to having another person read for you. On one hand, you may be tempted to gloss over difficult or unwelcome messages and focus on the most positive interpretation. On the other hand, a reader may interpret information based on their own frame of reference and miss things that the symbols are trying to communicate directly to your inner wisdom. Because experienced readers are much deeper and intuitive in their knowledge of the tool, I do recommend you consult a few. Then, go back and do your own reading on the same question and see what you get. In the interest of your own spiritual autonomy, you should be able to use the tools and tell yourself the truth about the message. But during the learning process, it does help to have many teachers.

These sections will include information about:

- How to set up the environment for a reading.

- How to select and use "keys" relevant to each system that will help you get into a magical frame of mind.

- How to shuffle, select, and/or cast the items required for divination using one or two simple but reliable reading techniques.

At first you won't have an intuitive understanding of each symbol, and even less of an understanding of how they modify or amplify each other to create a full reading. When you practice and become more fluent in the symbol language of the system, the overall tone of the reading will "hit" you and then the individual cards or Runes will fill in the rest.

For each system, I provide reference material to help you gain an initial interpretation. We will discuss how to use reference guides, and ultimately your own intuition, to interpret each symbol and then put the whole picture together to tell the story that answers the question.

There are three basic reasons to consult the Runes or cards:

- To answer our questions

- To learn how to approach difficult situations

- Because Spirit has something to say, and we want to hear it

Over time, practice and the development of intuition will enable you to know what the symbols mean individually and what story they tell in combination. Practice will also help you build trust in the system, as the results of your readings play out in experience.

Omens

Omen—events or conditions that are believed to foretell the future (such as assigning meaning to a black cat crossing your path)—are a kind of divination. In 2010, when a flock of geese flew over the crowd at Glen Beck's "Restore Honor" rally on the Washington DC Mall, he cited it as "God's flyover," indicating divine support. When Tim Tebow led the Denver Broncos to the January 2012 playoff win, his co-religionists considered it an affirmation of the power of Christian faith. But in 2010, the "Touchdown Jesus" statue in Monroe, Ohio, was destroyed by lightning and nobody commented much. One good rule to follow—either everything is a coincidence, or nothing is a coincidence. In any case, omens are an invitation to pay attention.

Exercise: Using omens

Get out your journal.

Consider a choice currently facing you—for example, whether to get up an hour early tomorrow and exercise, or stay up an hour now and watch one more episode of your favorite TV show.

Now set a condition—for example, "If the next commercial is the trailer for a new movie or for beer, I'll stay up. If it's for food, travel, or a nutritional supplement, I'll go to bed and get up to exercise."

Then see what happens. Set the condition again if you get none of those things.

The Pendulum

A pendulum is a talisman suspended from a chain. Pointed crystals are commonly used, but some people use the necklace they wear every day or suspend a ring or other personally meaningful object from the chain.

The pendulum is held by the end of the chain with the talisman hanging below. The user holds the pendulum over a board or sheet of paper containing the words Yes and No and possibly the numbers and alphabet, similar to a Ouija board.

A question is posed, and the movement of the pendulum indicates the answer by the direction it swings. It may spell out words or give numerical answers or respond to Yes or No questions.

Exercise: Using pendulums

First, think of a question about which you are conflicted or undecided that has some meaning in your life. For example, when faced with the choice of ending a long term-relationship, I asked the following questions:

- Is this relationship ready to end?

- Is it best for me if it does?

- Is it best for my partner if it does?

Next, make or acquire a pendulum. You can use a necklace you currently own, or you could go out and select a stone that appeals to you and attach a string to it. You can buy one, either from a metaphysical shop or online.

Next, on a sheet of paper, draw an equal-armed cross and write Yes at each end of the vertical axis and No at each end of the horizontal axis.

Decide which power you wish to invoke—your spirit guides, your Higher Self, patron Deity if you have one, or an ancestor. Ask that this entity support you with insight and knowledge.

"Tune" the pendulum to your energy by asking a few questions to which you know the answer, like "Is my hair (the color of your hair)?" "Am I male/female?" State that your intention is to tune the pendulum to your energy so your spirit resource knows you are not being frivolous.

Hold the pendulum above the page, close your eyes, and focus on your question. Note the movement of the pendulum. If it doesn't move, relax and try again.

Once you have tuned the pendulum by asking several "primer" questions, ask the question to which you really want to know the answer. Again, note the movement of the pendulum, and whether it correlates with the vertical axis (yes) or the horizontal axis (no).

Note the results and how you feel about them in your journal. You are not obligated to follow this advice—you have asked Spirit for information, and they have responded. You still have free will.

Whichever choice you make, note the results in your journal. If you really wanted to do Yes but Spirit said No (or vice-versa), what was the result of your ultimate choice?

Use the pendulum over the next week or so when you are faced with decisions or choices, and journal the results. If this tool feels comfortable and helpful, consider acquiring a more complex template and more resources on how to use the pendulum.

Chapter Seven

USING FUTHARK RUNES
FOR DIVINATION

*The Runes are an early form of western psychology concerned
with introspection, contemplation, and meditation.*
—Tyriel, *The Book of Rune Secrets*

THE FUTHARK RUNES DATE to the third century BCE and
evolved over hundreds of years in Northern Europe, including
modern day Germany and Scandinavia. Like the Tarot, the
Runes are a kind of living scripture, an arrangement of cosmic, unconscious, and conscious concepts and symbols that
can serve to show us where we stand right now and be a map
to show us the way forward They are named for the first six
Runes in the first row—Fehu, Uruz, Thurisaz, Ansuz, Raidho,
and Kenaz. In the following pages, I hope to introduce you
to the core concepts, history, and basic meaning of the Runes
and help you begin to build your divinatory muscles.

The god Odin is said to have "received" the Rune symbols
during a nine-day shamanic trance and fast. It is believed that

the knowledge of these symbols, and their spiritual significance, are "hard wired" into our collective memory.

Traditionally, attuning to the Runes is a very complex and deep spiritual process. Each Rune has a physical pose, a poem, and a song that combine to put the reader (known as Runester—or Vitki) in alignment with the cosmic significance of the Rune.

Traditional readings are highly ritualized, including the clothing, tools, and process one employs to cast and read the Runes. Understanding the seriousness and depth of the Runes is important. In practice, I approach Runic divination with the same frame of reference I do other magical workings: As long as their Spirit is shown the appropriate honor and respect, I have found Runes to be helpful and insightful partners. When I am unfocused, the messages are less clear. The energy is tangible when I am in alignment.

It is said that if anyone feels a strong attraction to the Runes, they probably held spiritual significance for the person in a way that goes beyond the experience in this life.

There are three major runic systems:

1. The foundational set is the Elder Futhark (named for the first seven Runes), consisting of twenty-four Runes

2. The Younger Futhark (sixteen Runes), which was developed around the seventh century CE

3. The Anglo-Saxon Futhark (thirty-three Runes), which yielded to the European alphabet through Christianization around 1000 CE

The systems differ in the number, shape, and, sometimes, name of the Runes. However, each of the Runes maintains its meaning and inner truth. And all three "are magically valid," according to Edred Thorsson, the author of *Futhark: A Handbook of Rune Magic*. For our purposes, we will use the Elder Futhark Runes.

Cosmology

The Runes are governed by the power of the Norse god Odin. Odin wants to be emulated, not worshipped. He is a god of personal strength, personal integrity, and accountability, and he expects the same from his followers.

It is said that he was the first to receive the wisdom of the Runes and was able to translate them into terms that could be understood by others. The myth states that Odin hung upside down in Yggdrasil, the yew tree that is the Norse Tree of Life, and entered what was essentially a shamanic trance in which the Runes and their meaning were given to him.

The Tree of Life has three roots, watered by three wells. The first of them connects back to Asgard, the home of the gods. The gods met daily at Urd's well, near the root. The three Norns, or Fates, lived by this well. Their names were Urd (Fate), Skuld (present), and Verdani (future). These names are important, as the Runes use these names to identify the positions of a three-Rune reading—Urd (what has led to this moment), Skuld (the influences most important now), and Verdani (what is likely to happen if you maintain current course and speed).

Some believe that Odin's "loss" of an eye is metaphorical, indicating that once you drink from the well of knowledge, you can no longer see from the perspective of ignorance, and knowledge of spirit leads you to see the mundane world in a different way. So Odin did trade one kind of sight for another.

Polarities like loyalty and betrayal, victory and defeat, power and weakness, fire and ice, creation and destruction appear throughout Norse mythology, so it is little wonder that Odin is a god of standing firm in who you are. The Runes are inclusive of all this and define a spiritual reality in which polarities are reconciled as connected, necessary both to each other and as part of the Soul's journey.

The Runes

Divination is an important function of the Runes, but not the first or only function. They are considered the foundation of magic and contain within them powerful, elemental forces. Odin's discovery/reception of the Runes while hanging from Yggdrasil for nine days was a revelation to him of the core concepts and principles of the universe.

They are, at once, representations of and "containers" for those forces. They are frequently used in charging objects, homes, and other artifacts with spiritual energy. They serve as a magical alphabet, facilitating communication of concepts and messages and strengthening spells as any magical alphabet does—through the power of the symbol and focusing the mind of the practitioner.

Their use alone or in "bindrunes"—combinations of symbols to denote meaning and power—is a frequent practice for protection, blessings, and spells. Runes may be found decorating weapons, garments, homes, and amulets for specific purposes, including protection, wealth, and relationships.

Each symbol represents a concept, for discussion and communication purposes, but it also contains within it the elemental energy of that concept. Each Rune has meaning at the personal level, the community level, and the universal level.

For example:

Othel

 Othel signifies prosperity and well-being, family, and community. These concepts are intertwined. If this Rune were to come up in the Verdani (future) position of a three-Rune reading for a person asking about his or her own affairs, it might signify these conditions coming into their life. If they were inquiring for the community or family, the meaning would be slightly different. If Othel appears in a reading or a position related to larger events, the meaning would be auspicious beyond the reader's own community.

However, Othel not only means prosperity, Othel *is* prosperity. So you could attract prosperity by wearing or carrying Othel after ritually charging the object on which it is written or engraved and asking for assistance, use it in an amulet, or carve it or attach it on your house. A reading would be divination. The amulet would be magic. Divination is a receptive activity. Magic is a projective activity.

Below are the twenty-four Runes of the Elder Futhark with interpretation.

ᚠ	ᚢ	ᚦ	ᚨ
FEHU	**URUZ**	**THURISAZ**	**ANSUZ**
1—F Wealth-success, Psychological power, Autonomy, New beginning	**2—U** Pattern, form, Organization, Vital energies, Freedom	**3—TH** Applied power, Challenge the status quo, Breaking Free	**4—A** Inspiration, Expression/Poetry, Transformation, Synthesis
ᚺ	ᚾ	ᛁ	ᛃ
HAGALL	**NAUDIZ**	**ISA**	**JERA**
9—H Crisis leading to transformation, Evolution, Seed of becoming, Transformation	**10—N** Resistance as that which makes you stronger, Resolve necessity, "Fire of need"	**11—I** Self-control Force of attraction Ego development Point of awareness	**12—J** Karmic reward, Relationship with environment, Patience Wheel of the Year
ᛏ	ᛒ	ᛗ	ᛗ
TIR, TIWAZ	**BERKANO, BEORC**	**EHWO/EHWAZ**	**MANNAZ**
17—T Justic, order, Judgment by power, Legal matters Greater Good	**18—B** Earth Mother Cycle of birth/death, rebirth Growth & Beauty	**19—E, EH** Teamwork Trust, loyalty Formal partnership Inner Harmony	**20—M** Intelligence Divine structure Conscious use of self

RAIDHO	KENAZ	GIFU	WUNJO
5—R	**6—K**	**7—G**	**8—W**
Hero's journey, Planned change, Preparation, Inner direction	Torch-light Learning Creativity Spirit forge	Generosity, Giving of self and material things, Energy exchange	Joy, Fellowship Harmony Relationships Business prosperity
EIHWAZ	**PERTHRO**	**ELHAZ**	**SOWILO**
13—E, I, Ei	**14—P**	**15—Z**	**16—S**
Enlightenment As above, so below Hidden influence Relationship with the numinous	Chance Personal Luck Prevail over randomness, The gambler	Protection Union with higher self, Imminent awakening	Solar wheel Phenomenal world Magical will Goal achievement
LAGAZ	**ING**	**DAGAZ**	**OTHEL**
21—L	**22—NG**	**23—D**	**24—O**
Unconscious Life energy of the universe Initiation, tests, Depth of spirit	Seed-potential Gestation Generation Cause & Effect	Total awakening Resolved Paradox Synchronicity Hope, happiness	Arriving home Well-being Family Community

How the Runes Are Organized

There are twenty-four Runes in the Elder Futhark. Each has three meanings:

- Its letter or phonetic value

- The concept it embodies

- The number that signifies both its place in the structure and its relationship to the other Runes.

The twenty-four Runes are organized in three Aetts or groups of eight. It is important to know that each of these three groups has an organizing principle and is named after one of the Norse gods. The top row is Freyja's Aett, the second row is Hagall's Aett, and the bottom row is Tyr's Aett.

Freyja's Aett: Inspiration, creation, fulfillment— beginnings and the cycle of life

Freyja was the most powerful of the Vanir, a group of older gods, and came to Asgard to teach magic to Odin.

Looking at Freyja's Aett as a spiritual progression, one notices the movement from Fehu, wealth and new beginnings, to Uruz, vitality and organization, then to Thurisaz, protection, power, and defense of what has been organized. This lays a new foundation for Ansuz, inspiration and synthesis. From here, Raidho introduces change and the hero's journey, to Kenaz, regeneration through sacrifice. This results in the gift of sharing and generosity (Gifu), which fosters and leads to authentic relationship and fulfillment in Wunjo, where the wealth of Fehu has been used rightly.

Hagall's Aett: Life experience

Hagall is the most powerful demon in Hel (the Norse Underworld) and is associated with conquest and acquisition, resistance and testing.

Hagall's Aett begins with the crisis leading to transformation (Hagall), leading to resistance and testing (Naudiz), which allows for ego development and learning self-control (Isa). Jera contains the principle of Karmic reward—the natural consequences of passing those tests. Eihwaz is the insight received from associating karmic results and the actions that led to them.

Perthro continues the learning process by teaching how you will receive joy, the process by which the past becomes the future, and Elhaz shows the way to the gods and spiritual insight.

Sowilo completes this phase with an understanding of the wheel of life and how one develops a magical will to achieve one's goals.

Tyr's Aett: Justice, governance, and community— including fulfillment of relationships

Tyr is the one-handed "Norse god of combat, victory, and heroic glory."

Tyr's Aett begins with Tyr, the Rune meaning justice and consolidation of victory through legal matters. Following victory is peace, which is the fertile ground for enlightenment. Beorc (Berkano) is the cycle of birth, death, and rebirth and is associated with the earth mother. Ehwaz (trust and loyalty, partnership) creates social structure, and Mannaz, the Divine structure of community. Lagaz provides the life energy of the universe that flows through that structure and builds to the potentiality and gestation of Ing, which also governs cause and effect. The birth or awakening after gestation leads to insight and joy, culminating in prosperity, well-being, and community.

BEGINNING RITUALS AND PRACTICES: THE RUNES

Acquiring Runes

Runes are available for purchase in most metaphysical shops and online. There are Runes made of polished stones with the symbols engraved on them and filled in with various colors of paint. Runes may also be in the form of staves (flat sticks) or discs cut from a tree branch. Traditionally, Runes are made from either wood or bone.

If you are serious about developing a relationship with the Runes, you will eventually make your own. The traditional form is to make the Runes of wood and ritually carve the symbols, filling the grooves with red natural dye or paint. I made a set of Runes from the branch of a cypress tree following the instructions in the book by Lisa Peschel listed in the bibliography. I find they work very well for me. I also bought a set of amethyst Runes online, and when they arrived, I did not connect with them, so I returned them.

Many Rune sets for sale will contain a blank or "Wurd" Rune—this was not originally part of the Germanic Rune tradition. It was invented by New Age American author Ralph Blum in 1982. It was intended to represent fate, or chance, or the influence of Spirit in the context of the reading. If you buy a set with a blank Rune, don't use it in context with this book. Simply put it aside in case you lose a Rune and need to make a replacement.

I do recommend making your own Runes. Rituals and processes for doing so are available in *Futhark: A Handbook of Rune Magic* and *Runecaster's Handbook* by Edred Thorsson.

Once you have the Runes you wish to work with, you should keep your Runes in a bag or box dedicated to that purpose.

If you can't get or make Runes right now, make a set from index cards. You can even add information about their number and meaning so they serve as both oracle and study guide. Please note, there are many applications of Rune magic, but we will deal only with readings.

Preparation
Cleansing and consecration

If you have made your Runes according to the principles and steps in the works above, they have been infused with your energy. As noted in the section on the Futhark system, they need no consecration, for the symbols are the cosmic principles they represent. If you purchase them, the physical material may retain the energy of others who have made and handled them, so I recommend cleansing and consecration using the following process: Prepare a sacred space. This can be a cleansed and consecrated room or, preferably, an outdoor space with trees.

There is a wide range of options for cleansing your space. I will offer two:

Sage and cedar: Both of these plants are known for having properties of purification and cleansing. Many people use sage to clear their own energy fields by lighting some and wafting the smoke around their bodies.

If you are able and wish to burn incense and herbs in the process of your work, dried sage and cedar are effective means of clearing space. If you can't or don't want to burn plant material for health or other reasons, you can obtain sage or cedar sprays from most metaphysical shops.

Put some sage and/or cedar in a dish and light it with a match or lighter.

Beginning in the east, walk around the space in which you are working counterclockwise, holding the intention that the smoke and the nature of the plants are helping clear the room of any stagnant or unfocused energy. You may even wish to say something like "with sage and cedar I cleanse and renew this space to support my work today." If you are using a spray, begin in the east and spray the mist into the air outward toward the perimeter of the room as you walk. In both cases, return to the center of the space and waft the smoke or spray toward the earth and then toward the sky.

Cleansing with visualization: Visualize a ball of brilliant white energy above your head. Imagine this energy flowing down into your body, through your chakras, into your hands. Using the palms of your hands, offer this light to all the corners and areas of the space, beginning in the east and moving around in a circle.

With either technique, be sure to hold the intention that the space will be cleared of any negativity or unfocused energy and prepared for your work.

1. Prepare an altar (a table or desk that you can use as your spiritual "work space"), traditionally facing north for working on spiritual issues or east for day-to-day questions. All tools should be present on the altar.

2. Perform a ritual to center, and disperse your own unfocused energy or energy not conducive to your working.

3. Cast or draw a sacred circle, going clockwise, to focus and contain the energy you raise.

4. Visualize removing the circle by releasing the energy in a counterclockwise fashion and cleanse the space again when you have finished your divination ritual.

Rune Readings

There are multiple ways to cast the Runes for divination. Here are a couple ways to use your Rune to receive guidance:

Single-rune readings

Draw a single Rune each morning after asking that it show you the dominant energy for your day. This will both give you guidance about your day and help you learn the Runes. The more you handle them and interact with them, the stronger your energy with them will be and the better you will get to know them.

For many weeks, I would ground, shield, and enter stillness, light the candles on my altar, and mix my Runes in their bag while saying the following incantation:

> *"Odin, Freyja, guide my hand*
> *to the Rune I'll understand.*
> *Will be my guidance for the day,*
> *to help me know what to do and say."*

Then I would pick the Rune, look up its meaning, and meditate on it briefly before starting my day.

Three-rune readings

The reading begins with your question. Put some thought and work into exactly what you want to know. Edred Thorsson describes the cosmology of this three-Rune reading in detail, but here are the basics:

- The first Rune you draw reveals the energy and events that have led to the situation for which you are seeking guidance.

- The second Rune reveals what is happening now spiritually and energetically, and how that is manifesting.

- The third Rune indicates the likely outcome if you maintain the current course.

For example, I asked this question about embarking on a new professional direction:

"How can I ensure the financial success of my new business?

After preparing as above, I put my hand in the Rune bag, mixed them up, and drew:

Beorc: Earth Mother; cycle of birth/death, rebirth; growth and beauty

Tir: Justice, order; judgment by arms; legal matters

Jera: Just reward; karmic reward; relationship with natural environment

As I take these Runes together, knowing the situation as I do, I come up with an overall theme to the reading and a sequence of development actions:

It is necessary to combine creative, innovative, and generative work with taking care of the legal, logistical, and formal aspects of running a business. If I balance these successfully, I will do well and I will earn in proportion to the effort I put out and the balance I achieve between "left brain" and "right brain" work.

This may seem obvious, but it made me realize I had been focusing on the generation and creation aspects of the business and needed to get my legal and procedural house in order.

The sequence of these Runes was very important to my interpretation as well. Beorc in the past position means doing the creative work to get things started, but it also points out that the cycle has turned to the birth of the new venture out of the death of the old way, and I need to let that go.

Tir in the present position means this is the time to focus on the logistical, legal, and accounting aspects of the business so I am set up for future success.

Jera in the future position means I will reap rewards based on my effort and my adherence to the values and principles inherent in the Rede, the Law of Three, and the Pyramid—the natural laws. By using the Futhark Runes for divination, you can see the guidance from Deity, or even from your Higher Self, depending on whom you decide to ask. The important part to remember is to be respectful of the Runes and to focus on your single question or intent as you cast the Runes. This process can be very helpful when you need help making decisions, need to know how a certain situation will play out, or even when you simply feel lost. Trust the Runes to guide you to knowledge greater than that which your conscious mind possesses, and allow yourself to be open-minded throughout the process.

Chapter Eight

THE TAROT

*"The Tarot reflects the opportunity that each individ-
ual has to visually see that life is a process of 'walking
the mystical path with practical feet,"*
—Angeles Arrien, *The Tarot Handbook: Practical
Application of Ancient Visual Symbols*

THE TAROT IS A card-based system of divination. The Reverend Donald Lewis describes it as a visual scripture that "contains within it all the secrets of the universe," a "visual map
of consciousness and a symbolic system" that offers personal,
professional, and spiritual insight, and "a kind of alphabet . . ."
that "offers a key to the Mysteries in a manner which is not
arbitrary and has not been read in." The meaning of the symbols is set. Their meaning to you is not. That is determined
by your question and the state of your Soul and mind when
consulting the tool.

There are hundreds of different decks from which to choose,
with vastly different and beautiful artwork. There are many
card-based oracles that are not the Tarot. You can spend hours

browsing in a physical or online metaphysical bookshop, and I encourage you to do your research to find the one that resonates with you. In this book, I will focus on the most commonly used Tarot deck, the Rider-Waite or Universal Waite deck.

Most decks include seventy-eight cards, divided into two sections:

1. Twenty-two cards called the Major Arcana, which contain rich symbolism and meaning. These cards in sequence trace the Soul's journey from creation through reunion with Deity and tell the story of that journey. In readings, these cards reflect the state of the Soul, the individual's development in this life, and major life themes and issues pertaining to the subject at hand.

2. Fifty-six cards called the Minor Arcana, divided into four suits, including an Ace, number cards two through ten, and court cards very similar to mundane playing cards with the addition of a court card called Page or Princess, in addition to the Knight (jack), Queen, and King. The suits respond to and communicate the energy of the four elements—usually Air for Swords, Wands (or Rods) for Fire, Cups for Water, and Pentacles (or Coins) for Earth. These cards tend to deal with more day-to-day or short-term happenings.

All decks consist of these two parts. Some have more or fewer cards and suits, some associate Air with Wands and Fire with Swords. We will use the Rider-Waite system in this discussion, which uses the original correspondences, as above.

The Tarot as the Hero's Journey

The Hero's journey begins when the child, or a person who is aware that there is more to existence than what is apparent through the five senses, becomes a seeker by setting out on their path. We are born into this life helpless, and our first needs are physical. Survival and development of the body as the tool our Soul will use to accomplish its purpose in this world are our primary objectives. As survival is assured, our mental and emotional development accelerate. We learn at an astounding rate how to interact with and navigate this world. We learn lessons about temperature and gravity, along with what we can and cannot put into our mouths. We build relationships—first with our immediate family, then with a widening circle of friends and acquaintances.

We take in an extraordinary amount of information and experience, and, somewhere along the way, we become aware of ourselves in a different way—it could be the first awakening of recognition that we do not stop at our skin, there is more to us than our senses can perceive, and there's something we should be doing.

At that moment, we realize we have to strike out on our own, and we begin the process of personal growth. It is then we become, in the words of the Tarot, the Fool. And this begins our journey and our tour through the Major Arcana.

This journey—the Soul's "learning curve"—is not an uninterrupted upward arc of learning, growth, and achievement. Life presents many decision points and hurdles. But the Soul does not begin unprepared, nor is the physical mind without skill. All the elements of fundamental learning—building the body; mastering mental concepts and disciplines; and the ability to form, nurture, and maintain relationships—are necessary ingredients to the spiritual journey to come.

The point of this spiritual journey is to discover, act upon, and fulfill the Soul's purpose in coming into this life and, ultimately, rejoining the Goddess.

The Major Arcana

The chart below summarizes the meaning of each card, both as its place in the Soul's journey and its possible implications in a reading.

Beginning: Creating the Life Plan

CARD	MEANING FOR THE JOURNEY	MEANING IN A READING
0 The Fool	The newly aware seeker, about to embark on the spiritual journey. The pack he carries means he has everything he needs for the journey. This card also counsels caution.	The seeker. New beginnings, old way has ended, new has not yet emerged. Leaping before you look. Risk taker. Avoid naïveté.
1 The Magician	The Magician represents developing Magical ability with the confidence to use it. The journey begins with a recognition of the seeker's power of will, ability to communicate, and creative energy.	Creative potential. Seen and unseen resources are available. Magical skills are present. Communication and persuasion are indicated.

CARD	MEANING FOR THE JOURNEY	MEANING IN A READING
2 The High Priestess	The joining of skill and knowledge with ethics and judgment. To leaven power with ethics. This card promises blessings and spiritual abundance, strength and support.	Spiritual awakening. Occult, deep thought. Mind, spirit. Power with values.
3 The Empress	Having flexed mental and Spiritual muscles and learned Spiritual lessons, the seeker recognizes the need to infuse the material with Spirit.	Creation, need for nurturing and patience. Integration. All abundance and happiness.
4 The Emperor	The seeker makes a plan. Integrated Spirit and matter permit an ethical strategy for moving forward.	Authority. Structure. Discipline. Someone who is in charge or willing to take charge.

Execution: Implementing the Life Plan

CARD	MEANING FOR THE JOURNEY	MEANING IN A READING
5 The Hierophant	Initiation into the Spiritual path. Becoming engaged in carrying out the plan for enlightenment. Hierophant = teacher.	Commitment—emotional or professional. Connection to the Divine. A teacher will appear.
6 The Lovers	Polarities appear. There is a need to reconcile seeming opposites. Trust your instincts about your true passion.	Relationships, a choice to be made between desirable alternatives or you will never be whole. Passion for relationship or work.
7 The Chariot	Duty and responsibility. Blending of polarities. Achieving victory through skill and persuasion. Creating solutions that are a blend of opposing perspectives, rather than one or the other.	Fighting for what is most important. Being strategic. Taking responsibility. Growing self-esteem through achievement.
8 Strength	Mental, emotional, or physical strength. Inner strength, victory over your impulses. Courage and daring mixed with discipline.	Maintain the courage of one's convictions. Assurance of inner strength and capability.

Reflection: Assessing Progress
in Fulfilling Your Purpose

CARD	MEANING FOR THE JOURNEY	MEANING IN A READING
9 The Hermit	Reflection, introspection. Pause on the journey to gather strength. Look deep within, seeking Spiritual guidance.	Time to reflect—lessons needed from going within. Much activity has yielded results. Keep what is worth keeping and release the rest.
10 Wheel of Fortune	Good luck, karmic payoff for invested effort. Rapid change, stroke of luck out of the blue. Gift from Fate. Destiny favoring you.	A gift from Fate. Your ship comes in. Stroke of good fortune. Benefit, favor.
11 Justice	Balance, consequences for material and spiritual actions. What the seeker has earned through effort. Karma. Needing to achieve or achieving justice.	The consequences of choices and actions are coming due, positive or negative. Possible arbitrated conflict.
12 The Hanged Man	Going deep within to gain insight through meditation, contemplation. Sacrifices. Surrender to destiny, maybe family or friends.	There has been a lot going on. A need to integrate learnings and experience. Can't move forward without pulling it all together. The path may change.

Transformation: Reaching a New Level

CARD	MEANING FOR THE JOURNEY	MEANING IN A READING
13 Death	Change. Passages. Destruction as prelude to rebirth. Ending.	Something is changing. Something old is ending, to make way for the new.
14 Temperance	Balance, tempering, joining polarities. Blending male/female, will and spirit, with each remaining unique. Reconciling opposites.	Resolving polarities—discovering a way to find the "both/and" rather than the "either/or." Unsettled time when the rules are suspended.
15 The Devil	Bondage, oppression. Addiction (emotional or physical). Overcoming perceived chains that can be moved aside.	Self-examination—what is really holding you back? How are you tying yourself down? Master assertive energy. Self-limitation.
16 The Tower	Chaos, confusion. Destruction of old constructs. Tearing the veil off the false and illusory. Exposing the truth as the basis for rebuilding. Arguments, problems, accidents.	Old structures are crumbling; the truth will be exposed. Not under questioner's control.

Integration: Releasing and Becoming

CARD	MEANING FOR THE JOURNEY	MEANING IN A READING
17 The Star	Hope and joy, healing to come. Knowledge and possibilities. Spiritual insight, clearing of vision through spiritual practices.	There is hope for the situation or person. This is not certain, but with the right focus it is possible. The possibilities for positive outcome are strong.
18 The Moon	Disturbance, mental tension. Not seeing the truth, believing distortions. In the grip of one's shadow. Journeying to the unconscious. Caught between fear and illusion. Wandering confused.	Illusion must be overcome by confronting fear and ego. The unconscious holds much knowledge but can be a snare. Confusion and indecision.
19 The Sun	Prosperity. Renewal, rebirth of true self. Awakening to spiritual reality. Overcoming illusion through material action.	The battle has been won. Illusion has been overcome. The situation is reborn, new life emerging.
20 Judgment	Face what you have to face, release old habits and constructs. Get on with it. Realization, making the choice to fulfill your destiny.	Objective self-judgment. Taking stock of lessons learned, atoning for mistakes. Moving on.

Fulfillment

CARD	MEANING FOR THE JOURNEY	MEANING IN A READING
21 The World	Everything comes together. Dreams, hopes fulfilled. All is yours.	Wish will be fulfilled, situation will be righted. The new beginning is fully realized.

Minor Arcana

On the following page is a chart showing the basic definitions of the cards in the Minor Arcana. These cards have more to do with daily life—in the areas of thought (Swords), will and purpose (Wands), emotion and relationships (Cups), and material prosperity (Pentacles), or Air, Fire, Water, and Earth, respectively. Each number or court card carries its own significance as well.

The Minor Arcana

	SWORDS Air/Thought	WANDS Fire/Will	CUPS Water/ Emotion	PENTACLES Earth/ Physical, Material
ACE Positive qualities of guiding element.	Focused, powerful intellect. Beginning of a project or intellectual pursuit. Decision.	Energetic, passionate, eager to embrace something new. Courageous and confident, moving forward.	Happiness, experiencing love and emotions intensely. Spiritual and emotional fulfillment.	Grounded, centered, build a foundation and do excellent work. Integration, prosperity.
TWO Duality—manifestation.	Partnership. Need for collaboration and finding opportunities for mutual gain.	Original and creative, bold and daring. Achievement through partnership. Commands others' attention and respect.	Open exchange with others. Learning about each other. Romantic attraction. A new or key relationship.	Building reputation through quality and quantity of work. Long hours. Working with others.
THREE Public expression of elemental energy.	Hidden feelings are expressed. Possible end, major change, separation of important relationship.	Effort and risk, leadership and commitment pay off as your "ship comes in." Coach or mentor appears.	Joyful celebration with a group—family or otherwise. Building community.	Reputation leads to more work, building an enterprise. Possible investors/patrons.
FOUR Element at rest—stable, in balance.	Need for renewal and reflection. Back to basics, recharge batteries.	Celebrating a victory/event—pausing to savor the outcome of hard work.	Withdrawal. Become introspective, contemplative. Consolidation.	Resisting change. Holding on too tight. Let go and let flow.
FIVE Change/transformation in the formerly stable situation. Disruption.	Hostility, acting for self, winning at someone's expense, Restrained by others.	Energetic opposition arises from self and others. Difficulties, disagreements. Dissent.	Sorrow, regret. Possible loss. Feeling hopeless.	Downturn in business, health, other conditions. Feeling isolated and rejected. Loss.

	SWORDS Air/Thought	WANDS Fire/Will	CUPS Water/ Emotion	PENTACLES Earth/ Physical, Material
SIX Resolution and harmony after change/ disruption.	Winding down, possible regret, depression. Taking stock. Pride. Victory. Working through the challenges at five leads to resolution and achievement. Longing for "good old days," in the aftermath of loss or conflict. Start over.	Fulfillment of mission on way to a larger purpose, completion of a step along the path. Learning and growth have been achieved from trials and effort.	Harmony has been achieved in relationships— difficulties have been overcome. All is ready to move into a new phase of change and growth.	Leadership opportunity—need to restore balance. Putting wealth in motion toward a goal. Possible benefactor.
SEVEN Work to integrate lessons learned; new insights and growth.	A difficult struggle that can be successfully resolved.	Confident and steadfast, have the resolve to stay the course. Hard work leads to success.	Recognition of one's emotional needs and wants, and stuck among too many desirable choices. Overcoming illusion.	Sort out true opportunities for growth. Nurture things until they come to fruition. Decisions to be made.
EIGHT Energy of the element at its most intense.	Stuck—conflict with no easy way out. Restrained, no wiggle room.	Sudden changes, important new information, accelerated progress toward a goal.	Blowing things out of proportion.	Focus and dedication to mastering talents and completing projects with excellence.
NINE Elemental energy in highest expression.	Inner conflict and remorse. Conflict ended, but hard on self for outcome. Anxiety, stress.	True use of "will power." Courage to stay the course and gut it out in the face of resistance.	Manifestation of emotional/ spiritual desires— Get what you most want. Energy, creativity, relationships on the increase.	Using good judgment. Self discipline—living autonomously.
TEN Bringing the situation to a resolution.	Resolution—the situation is complete, time to move on.	Passion has been realized, difficulties overcome. Have courage. Change is imminent.	Experience emotional stability and a permanent, foundational sense of joy.	Time to enjoy what one has earned— desired manifestation has been realized or soon will be.

Court Cards—Representing people currently present or entering the situation, or the querent.

	SWORDS Air/Thought	WANDS Fire/Will	CUPS Water/ Emotion	PENTACLES Earth/ Physical, Material
PAGE/ PRINCESS Message arriving. Ethical, rational approach indicated. Portent of change.	Resiliency in the face of resistance. A new idea or way of thinking has arrived or is on the horizon. May be disruptive but will change the paradigm.	Taking creative approaches, inspiring others through passion, enthusiasm, and force of personality.	Children. New love or breakup, intense emotional situation	Realizing goals, getting results. Building trust and a reputation for delivering. Resist the obvious choice.
KNIGHT/ PRINCE Excessive energy—in thought, action.	Forceful, opinionated, verbal. Rational to the exclusion of emotion. Cold, critical. Self-interest.	Passionate, volatile, impetuous. Extroverted, high energy, not liking to be thwarted.	Volatile emotional person or situation— possible change in relationship.	Lots of things in motion, frenetic activity but with a purpose. May fear failing.
QUEEN Internal expression of elemental energy.	Directness balanced with wisdom and the larger picture. Sees through deception.	A diva—can be radiant, warm, energetic, and inspiring or bossy, domineering, and intimidating.	Focus on deeper meaning of things, compassion and sensitivity shown. Joy.	Hospitable, practical, warm, and generous. Provides love and support for your efforts.
KING Extroverted energy of the element in manifestation.	The objective judge— reason, rationality expressed in decisions and actions.	Charismatic, impatient, innovative, high-energy leader. Maybe a preacher or politician. May preen.	Caring, diplomatic, emotionally strong student of humanity. Servant leader.	Financial success, integrity, goal achievement, translating ideas to reality.

Resources: "Thirteen's Tarot Card Meanings"; Learning the Tarot; Lessons in the Correllian Tradition, Second Degree.

Beginning Rituals and Practices: Tarot
Buying cards

It can be confusing. There are dozens of Tarot card decks available, with designs and formats ranging from the traditional Rider-Waite and Thoth Decks to dragon- to crystal- to herb-oriented decks as well as African, Italian, Chinese, Japanese, Native American, and other themed decks. In addition, there are multiple oracles available, such as the Medicine Cards that are not based on the Tarot at all.

Most metaphysical supply stores stock Tarot cards and have demonstration decks available. Select a Major Arcanum and see which artwork appeals to you. Get a sense for the energy of the design, and when you find yourself attracted to one, go with your intuition. Most people who use Tarot own multiple decks.

The story about my fortuitous late-night motorcycle ride actually began about a month earlier, when I was buying my cards in preparation for a Tarot course. I chose the Moon card as the one to compare the decks. The Tarot reader and store owner came over and said, "We were just discussing the Moon card." The reader explained the imagery on the card this way:

> The path of spiritual enlightenment—the journey
> back to the Goddess—lies before the seeker. This

is the path of insight through spiritual growth and practice. The card itself portrays a crawfish climbing out of water toward a path between two dogs. Past the two dogs are two towers, with the moon shining over the scene. The path begins at the water, the depths of spiritual knowledge. Behind the seeker is a crawfish, a serpent, blocking the way back. No going back, once you step on this path. The road itself—leading directly to the destination—the Moon, the Goddess.

However, on the left and right are two dogs. The one on the left is tame. The one on the right is wildness, passion, risk in the extreme—the temptation to leave the path for intensity of experience. The path itself is a balance between the passionate and the mundane, between safety and challenge. It is the learned lesson of calculated risk—motivation, passion in the service of mind and heart.

Halfway up the path are two towers. My understanding is the tower on the left represents Pride, the Tower on the right represents Fear. When we reach this point in our journey, the entities in these towers engage us in conversation. Pride wants us to protect our egos from embarrassment and failure. Fear wants us to avoid the wildness and consequences of our passion. And both tell us, each in its own way, that it is not safe to continue. We argue, we bargain, we take one side and then the other. And they will engage us forever, and keep us right there, as long as we let them.

The journey is initiated when we are awakened to it by Spirit. And we are ultimately saved from the battle of Pride and Fear when Spirit comes to us and asks why we are engaging with them. When we recount their arguments, Spirit says, "Don't you see? They can't help or hinder you. Their purpose is to keep you engaged so you do not progress beyond them."

Pride and fear are the two weapons of the ego. And we are in grave danger if we do not escape them, because they are being used as tools to keep us where we are.

In my story, the traffic behind me and the need to join my family prevented me from turning around. No going back, once you step on this path, as the reader had said. The road itself—clear and straight, leading directly to the destination—was the Oregon Coast. The road represents the known, the safe, the avoidance of risk—the temptation to leave the path for the "safety" of the mundane, and ignorance.

For me, the tame dog was the double yellow line and oncoming traffic, the need to stay rigorously safe from collision and observe the boundaries. Follow the rules. The second dog—the wild one—was the natural forest with all its wildlife and potential to engage me at any moment. This potential increased when the "Elk crossing" signs began to appear. Deer might jump out in front of me. Elk are likely to decide they don't like my motorcycle and do something about it.

Thanks to the actual Moon's appearance (activating my Higher Self's ability to help me see the situation differently), my insight caused me to refocus on the journey and be vigilant but determined to move forward. I was cautious but not terrified any longer.

I had essentially picked the Moon card as a single-card reading for myself and got an expert interpretation. This information was directly relevant to my life at the time. So the adventure begins as you get your cards. In fact, it has already begun.

Cleansing and Charging the Cards

The next step is to cleanse and charge your cards. This removes any unfocused energy or the energetic imprint of others who may have handled them. It also begins to focus your intention and build your relationship with the deck. It alerts Spirit that you are opening a communication channel. And it begins the process of seeing, learning, and interacting with the imagery and themes of the cards.

Preparing your cards

Cleansing and consecration are the first steps. This serves two purposes. First, just as it was with the Futhark Runes, this aligns the energy of the cards with your energy, so that they are attuned to you and vice versa. This improves communication. Second, it is a sign to Spirit that you are taking this seriously and asking their help in the communication process.

You may already have ways of cleansing ritual tools and other objects and aligning with your own spirit guides and helpers. Here is my process: I smudge myself with sage or sweetgrass; ground, shield, and infuse my aura with light; use

Reiki symbols and self-Reiki to start the flow of energy. Then I take the cards and do the same:

> *Smudging with sage or sweetgrass*: Light some sage in a burning dish and move the cards around in the smoke for as long as it feels right.

> *Visualizing cleansing and consecration*: I hold the cards in my left hand and visualize yellow light bathing them from the palm of my right hand as I hold it over the cards. I visualize them being cleansed of all unfocused or negative energy and any leftovers from prior reading. Then I visualize blue light bathing them from my right palm, asking that they be consecrated for this purpose and the Highest Good.

Regular maintenance

Every few months, infuse with full-moon energy: When it feels right to do so, cleanse the cards and then put them out for the three nights of the full-moon period and ask that they be infused with that energy.

Framing Your Question and Choosing a Reading Format

There are big questions and small questions—strategic questions, life direction questions, and day-to-day tactical questions. There are also time-bound questions, from "what is my life purpose and path?" to whether or not to interview for a specific job. The nature and scope of the question will help dictate the reading you choose to perform. We will start with the tactical.

Single-card readings: What can I expect today?

Many Tarot readers will select a single card in the morning to understand the influence that will be operating that day. I did this regularly for a while and drew cards like:

> *Inverted Three of Cups*: Happiness and celebration, but turned upside down. I went into work and discovered we were gathering to help someone deal with the grief of the sudden loss of a family member.

> *The Tower*: This card indicates chaos and the disruption of an old way of living, including loss of trust and stability of institutions and structures. I found this card coming up on days that turned out to include changes in structure and expectations at work, and disruption of my plans in other areas.

> *Four of Pentacles*: This is the "miser" card—someone focused on protecting material wealth and possessions. This card came up consistently for a while, and I realized I was in a pattern of focusing on a mind-set of security and scarcity rather than abundance.

Again, this is not your daily doom exercise. This is an indication of the energy that is around you or that you are carrying. And it is your choice how to deal with or respond to that energy.

Three-card readings: What's going on here?

A decision needs to be made. A difficult choice looms. A situation has arisen and you can't see your way out.

A good way to address these questions, especially in the beginning, is with a three-card, past-present-future reading by choosing three cards and laying them out in a straight, horizontal line. Just as we practiced with the Futhark Runes, the card on the far left is the past, the card in the middle is the present, and the card on the far right represents the future.

For example, the questioner asked:

"What should I do about this relationship that feels like it is not working?"

PAST—*Page of Swords*: I have been resilient in the face of resistance. Diplomatic, willing to empathize and see both sides. This is definitely how I had participated in the relationship.

PRESENT—*Five of Cups*: Disappointment and sorrow, feeling hopeless. This is an accurate statement of my state of mind at the time of the reading, and a natural reaction to focusing on someone else's needs to the exclusion of my own.

FUTURE—*Ten of Cups*: Personal fulfillment and happiness. If I can recognize and act upon the fact that both of us are focusing on the other person's needs and no one is focusing on mine, I can reset appropriate boundaries and get what I want either within the relationship or, if necessary, by dissolving it and moving on.

Sometimes these things are difficult to accept, but generally there is a message that something in the situation is controllable by you, and the reading gives you an indication of both what may be going on and the kind of action you might take. We may not always be able to control what comes at us, but we can always choose how to respond. And these readings can give you a sense of the best energy to bring to the situation.

Past-present-future is only one of many ways you can use a three-card reading. You can use the three cards to represent where you are in the situation, what's working for you, and what's working against you—or any three elements of a dilemma or question. As long as you focus clearly, you will get meaningful information.

As you practice, the three-card reading can also be done at the beginning of each day to get a more in-depth view of the forces and influences around you. In this case, you would not think of past, present, and future, but do the following:

- Turn over each card, and note the message it sends.

- Think about how those messages combine into a theme or "story."

Complex readings: *The big questions or "I need more information"*

Big questions do not necessarily require complex readings, but you will probably want more detail. For example, if the relationship question above was not resolved and began to move to a more serious situation, you might do a more complex reading with more cards to get further information. My favorite complex reading is the Celtic Cross.

About Inverted Cards

As you use your cards, you will sometimes find that they are inverted or upside down when you turn them over. In single-card readings, it is common to simply read the card the same way in either direction. In more complex readings, however, the inverted card indicates that the energy it represents has been weakened or is in the process of transition. Please see the example below.

Celtic Cross

While a three-card reading may suffice for the moment, if you want additional information, I suggest using the Celtic Cross spread. This reading, and the others briefly described, provide more depth and a longer-range view.

There are many versions of this reading. The diagram below is how I usually perform this card layout, though there are many variations.

Celtic Cross

CARD 1:
What is the essence of the question?

CARD 2:

What are the obstacles the questioner is facing? What's crossing with you?

CARD 3:

What has happened in the past to lead to this point?

CARD 4:

What does the immediate future hold?

CARD 5:

What is the inner desire operating here?

CARD 6:

What is the best that can be hoped for?

CARD 7:

Where is the questioner now with regard to the situation?

CARD 8:

What conditions are surrounding the questioner?

CARD 9:

What are the emotions operating right now?

CARD 10:

What is the most likely outcome?

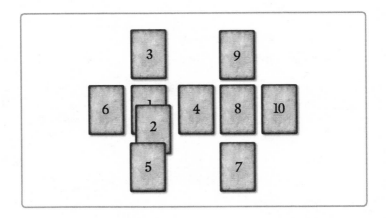

There are other readings that cover a year and can give even more information. But using these three readings will answer most questions and allow you to gain an understanding of the meaning of each card as well as how they influence each other.

Experiment and try things. Below is a sample Celtic Cross reading to illustrate how the cards come together to answer a question.

A Sample Celtic Cross Reading

The questioner was in a tumultuous and difficult relationship where both parties loved each other but found themselves increasingly at odds. Unfortunate things had been said by both and there was some concern about whether they could recover the relationship or not. The questioner simply asked if it should be ended.

Since the cards provide direction but do not compel anything, the reading is information regarding the forces at work in the situation. The notes to the right indicate what the cards and symbols meant to the questioner.

Card Meaning

1	King of Swords (Inverted)	**What is the essence of the question?** There is declining energy to communicate and find solutions. There is irrational thinking and expression going on. One or both are not being fully honest and truthful.
2	The Moon (Inverted)	**What are the obstacles facing the questioner?** There have been confusion and stories being made up about the situation. The difficulties that are perceived may not be fully illusory—there may be some truth to the concerns causing the parties to hold back.
3	9 of Pentacles (Inverted)	**What has happened in the past to lead to this point?** The questioner has lacked self-discipline and restraint. Judgment has not been good. Lack of self-control has led to hurt and confusion.
4	4 of Swords	**What does the immediate future hold?** An opportunity to step back and consider, think things over, rest, and get perspective. There is a need to center and rebuild strength and energy. Time to return to basics, recharge.
5	Judgment	**What is the inner desire operating now?** Take stock of lessons learned—release what is restraining you, make the choice to fulfill your purpose. Forgive and be forgiven. The questioner wants to put everything on the table, resolve it, and forgive it.

6	High Priestess	**What is the best that can be hoped for?** An awakening of deep understanding, through patience and allowing the answer to emerge. This is a spiritual issue and will be addressed by ethical treatment and through spiritual awareness rather than a new mental understanding. A fundamental shift in the energy of the relationship toward values-based living, with blessings and strength from the Goddess.
7	Wheel of Fortune (Inverted)	**Where is the questioner now with regard to the situation?** The energy of good fortune has been diminished. Luck is still present, but material, spiritual, and emotional good fortune are at a low point. Disaster has not struck, but life has gone a bit gray.
8	7 of Cups	**What conditions are surrounding the questioner?** Too many options are available—there is a choice between the dynamics of this relationship and everything else—nothing settled or rooted, no clear other choice. The questioner is engaging in wishful thinking and may be fooling himself about the severity of the problem. He is not aware of, or attending to, his own emotional needs, perhaps fixated on "fixing" the relationship by attending to the other person.
9	King of Wands	**What are the emotions operating right now?** Desire to create drama, force the issue, be bold. Extroversion and high energy create impatience. Belief in the questioner's own charisma to carry the day.
10	Page of Pentacles	**What is the most likely outcome?** Dreams come true. Goals are realized, trust and a reputation for keeping commitments are built. Prosperity, wealth, and abundance arrive. In the context of the question, a fulfilling, emotionally rich relationship will likely be realized if the conditions and tests in the other cards are addressed.

Summary

You always have free will. So even though the questioner was seeking a "yes" or "no" answer, he got sufficient information to allow him to make a decision.

Mistakes have been made in this relationship, by both parties. But the questioner's intensity and lack of self-discipline have led him to blurt things out and essentially go on the attack emotionally. This has led to holding back—declining energy in the relationship and confusion regarding what is felt and what is true. There has been some mild betrayal and breaking of trust.

The two people involved are now faced with the opportunity to reevaluate, take stock, and try to find new ways to relate to each other.

If they do so successfully, they will learn a great deal about themselves in the short term, and these lessons can strengthen the relationship in the long term if they choose to remain together and if they remain open to the messages of Spirit and the lessons of forgiveness.

If they navigate this territory well, their dreams will come true.

Based upon this reading, the questioner decided that he would remain in the relationship and do his best to allow space and time to heal the damage done.

Using Runes and Tarot to Find Your Path

To plan your path to anywhere, you must define two things—your starting point and your destination. So let's begin with where you are, and I suggest using one of the two divination methods mentioned previously (Tarot or Futhark Runes) or having a reading done professionally to consult your inner or higher wisdom on the following question:

What conditions, people, and practices in my life are currently serving my spiritual growth, and what should be released?

Depending on the results you get, you may find you need to split this into two readings.

Approach #1: Go get a professional reading

- Research psychics at metaphysical bookstores, psychic fairs, and in private practice.

- Call and connect with the few who seem to fit your personality and need.

- Schedule a reading, offering the question above.

I highly recommend audio recording the reading because when you try to recall it later, you will find you are not at the same energetic place you were when the reading occurred and will likely forget most of it.

Review the recording and write for a while in your journal about how the reading reflects the conditions in your life that are presently fulfilling for you and those you wish to release, change, or bring to yourself.

Approach #2: Your own three-Rune or -card reading

- Center yourself, then enter your meditative/ still level of awareness.

- Prepare your cards and the setting in whatever way works for you.

- Set the intention to ask the Oracle (Higher Self/Deity/etc.) where you have been on your spiritual path, where you are now, and the likely outcome in the future.

- Draw the three cards or Runes, interpret them using the sources you trust, and make notes on the answers.

Let's start with the first two Runes/cards. Using the questions below as a guide, write for a while in your journal about how the reading reflects the conditions in your life that are presently fulfilling for you and those you wish to release, change, or bring to yourself.

- To what extent are your current spiritual practice, your work, and your relationships providing you with joy, optimism, fulfillment, and peace?

- Where in your body and mind do you feel the longing or desire to pursue a new path? What does it feel like?

- To what extent are your values, heart, and Soul engaged by your work?

- To what extent are your values, heart, and Soul fed by your relationships?

Elaborate to develop a full story of your starting point.

Approach #3: Association
This approach may be best if you don't yet feel comfortable working with Runes or Tarot cards, either by yourself or with

the help of a professional. This is a very "beginner-friendly" approach to divination on this question.

Acquire or look online for a collection of images—nature, people, city streets, and sporting events—images of all kinds.

Read through the questions below and select an image that evokes the feelings, conditions, and desires of where you are now in your search.

In your journal, write down three ways in which the image reflects your current state.

As in the reading, use the questions below as a guide and write for a while about how your interpretation of the image reflects the conditions in your life that are presently fulfilling for you and those you wish to release, change, or bring to yourself.

- To what extent are your current spiritual practice, your work, and your relationships providing you with joy, optimism, fulfillment and peace?

- Where in your body and mind do you feel the longing or desire to pursue a new path? What does it feel like?

- To what extent are your values, heart, and Soul engaged by your work?

- To what extent are your values, heart, and Soul fed by your relationships?

In your journal, write a letter to Spirit to develop your learnings into a full story of your starting point—where are you now that leads you to undertake this journey? Give this sufficient time to make sure you feel you have accurately described your current situation. In a day or so, proceed to the next question: Where are you going?

Where Are You Now: Example

The following statements were based on the association method—finding photographs that evoked the feelings and conditions facing the individual at the start of their work.

The photo was an artistic illustration of a man crawling out from under the edge of a bubble that housed a mundane world of roads and houses and people, into a fantasy land of sparkling orbs, trees, and faeries.

> I am caught between worlds—one that is enclosed by a bubble and includes all the trappings and obligations, and one that is expansive, open, breathing, and enlightened. I am on my knees, unable to move forward. I'm hobbled by external obligations, trapped by them as if in a pillory, helpless to move as everyone passes by me, paying the price for failing to meet their expectations. I am besieged and overwhelmed by priorities that take all my time, leaving me no room for my own growth and development. I've lost my way and feel I can see but not reach the bright path. Everything happens above me, and I am lost in mists of uncertainty.

This was very high level and poetic, and so a three-Rune reading was used to get a sense of what has led to this place, where the situation is right now, and the likely future if things continue on their current course and speed:

Rune in the Past position: Elhaz (Z)

Meaning: Protection, union with higher self, imminent awakening

Interpretation: Earlier on in my search, I encountered Divine forces for which I was not prepared, and with insufficient preparation, I have wielded them in a way that made my own situation more difficult. So I tried blocking them out,

 pulling the covers over my head and hoping they would go away, but thereby cut myself off from a critical source of inspiration and insight. Hence, I felt spiritually blind and deaf.

Rune in the Present position: Lagaz (L)

Meaning: Unconscious, life energy of the universe, initiation, tests, depth of spirit

Interpretation: I am in a state of transition from one way of being to another. This will involve difficult tests, but I have the vital energy to withstand them. I must act and be in control of myself. I need to go deep into the dynamic spiritual waters to grow.

Rune in the Future position: Ehwaz (Eh)

Meaning: Teamwork, trust, loyalty, formal partnership, inner harmony

 Interpretation: Harmony and teamwork are in the future, with good results. There will be a

partner—a mentor or spouse. Trust and loyalty will be built, and a partnership will result.

Combining these two methods of divination (association and Futhark Runes) gives an excellent picture of this person's current situation. Out of the turmoil of significant change, decisions and actions have been taken that have now led to a period of tests and difficulties.

Chapter Nine

MANIFESTATION: FOCUSING AND DIRECTING ENERGY

*What you think, and what you feel, and what manifests, is
always a match, every single time. No exceptions.*
—Esther Hicks

MANIFESTING ANYTHING—prosperity, emotional connections, events, outcomes—is a process of affirmatively focusing
and directing energy in the direction of your goal.

Some things we might wish to manifest are best accom-
plished using mundane techniques—for example, doing ritual to help you learn to play the piano may help establish
your mind-set for doing so, but ultimately you will have to
study and practice. Similarly, if you are having difficulty in
a relationship or a job, performing rituals may help you get
into a more forgiving mind-set, but you will also have to do
the interpersonal work required. However, if you have tried to
address these things, and you feel blocked in a way you don't
understand, these techniques can be very helpful in removing

the blocks. This, however, means your intention is about reducing your own resistance rather than about the piano, the job, or the relationship. And reducing your resistance will support your Soul's growth in other areas. The Universe will always answer at the level of the root cause of your concern.

The key ingredients for manifesting your goals are a clear intention—a picture in your mind of the desired outcome; a method of engaging the assistance of what you understand to be the powers in the Universe to which you relate most strongly; and an act of expressing your intention to the Universe that focuses and releases the energy of your intention so that your desire will be manifested.

The preparation steps are effective in both clearing the space and your mind of other energy and thoughts, and getting the attention of all supporting entities and telling them that there is a person here with work to be done.

This stuff works.

While working to manifest your intentions, it is extremely important to bear in mind the following:

- If your intent is not clear, you will likely not be successful, because the energy won't know where to go.

- If your Higher Self, your Soul, does not agree that your desire is for your highest good, nothing may happen, or something else may happen that you did not expect.

- If you insist, you may get what you asked for. So it is important to be sure you really want it.

It is inappropriate and unethical to perform these acts of manifestation to manipulate the behavior, feelings, or life circumstances of another person. For example, if you are looking for an intimate relationship, you might do a spell to make yourself more attractive to your preferred gender, which would potentially bring you the best partner for you. You would never perform a ritual to get someone specific to fall in love with you, which would violate their individual autonomy.

You can use these tools and techniques to help you focus energy on any outcome, but for our purposes I suggest selecting elements of your vision for your spiritual path that you want to attract into your life, or things you need to release to allow yourself to move forward.

The Steps

Ground, release, center using the process discussed in the previous chapter.

Cleanse the space in which you are working. Remember you can burn sage and cedar to cleanse this space, or use the visualization technique.

Establish sacred space. To establish a sacred space, visualize a white light above your head. Imagine it flowing down to your heart area. Visualize a ball of light forming in the center of your chest, then widening into a disc that begins to spin clockwise, becoming bigger until it reaches the limits of the space. Then imagine it growing vertically into a sphere of white, protective light surrounding your working area. Say something like, "I am now in Sacred Space. Only good and loving things can enter or happen here."

Invoke your Higher Self and Guides and Divine assistance.

Based on your work earlier in this book, you may have identified your personal cosmology—whom or what you connect with when you think of Deity, and the guides, angels, or ascended masters you may have worked with in the past.

Invoking them means calling them by name and asking that they be present to help you in this work. It is customary to formally bid them hello and welcome. Think through whom you will invoke, and in what order, because you should release them in the end in the reverse order in which they were invoked.

Do not invoke specific deities unless you have done the research to know their nature, what they offer, and how to honor them.

- Perform your act of manifestation.

- Thank and release Deity, Elements, Guides, and Higher Self in the reverse order in which you invoked them.

- Release Sacred Space by visualizing it dissolving and saying, "The circle is open, but never broken."

- Cleanse and release excess energy.

- Ground, release, center.

- Journal what you did and why.

- See what happens.

Truthfully, you do not need the trappings of Magic to focus and direct energy. However, they can serve to put you in the Magical frame of mind. As you continue on your path, you will read and research many methods and structures for manifestation. These simple techniques are intended to help you experience the process of deliberately forming an intent and focusing energy on making it happen.

Paper-Burning Manifestation Technique

To perform this second manifestation technique, you will need a candle or two, a slip of paper for each intention, and a dish into which you can place the burning paper. Also, have a knife or other implement you can use to move the paper around as it burns so it burns completely.

Before beginning, spend some time becoming very clear about your desired outcome. Write the key phrases on a slip of paper. For example:

- To find work that uses my creativity, passion, and skills, or

- To reduce fear, grief, or loss

For releasing, use a black candle. For manifesting, use a white candle.

After grounding, clearing, and releasing for yourself, cleansing your space, consecrating it, and invoking your Divine assistance:

- Light your candle.

- Take the slip of paper and read it aloud.

State your purpose, visualizing the helpers you have invoked, crumple the paper slightly, light it in the candle flame, and say, for example:

> "As this paper burns, the work that best uses my creativity, passion, and skills is coming to me. I expect this, I am grateful for it, I see it manifesting in my life now. I ask this for the good of all, with harm toward none, that all may be blessed. May it be so."

If you are releasing rather than manifesting, make sure to change the invocation accordingly.

Be sure to drop the paper in the dish to finish burning before you scorch yourself.

Burning-Candle Manifestation Technique

You will need a candle of a color that matches your intent (you can find many guides for candle colors online, in metaphysical book stores, etc.; but you can also just use the ones that speak to you and feel aligned with your intention), a candle holder, and lighter.

Again, before beginning, spend some time becoming very clear about your desired outcome.

After grounding, clearing, and releasing for yourself, cleansing your space, consecrating it, and invoking your Divine assistance:

- Light some sage or cedar, and pass the candle through the smoke to release any prior associations or stored energy or intention.

- Do the same with the lighter you will use to light the candle, and the candle holder.

- Hold the candle between your palms, and visualize a ball of energy surrounding the candle.

- Charge the candle with your intention within this ball of energy. For example, you might use an orange candle for the manifestation of work that uses your creativity, passion, and skills because work is associated with prosperity and orange is the color of the sacral chakra, which governs creativity, passion, and joy.

Place the candle in its holder. As you do so, state out loud what you want to attract. Be sure your intention is clear. For example:

"As this candle burns, so is the energy released to attract to me the work that best uses my creativity, passion, and skills. I ask for this, I am grateful for it, I manifest this in my life now. I ask this for the good of all, with harm toward none, that all may be blessed. May it be so."

Light the candle. If you can allow the candle to burn down completely in a safe manner, then do so. If you will have to extinguish it when you leave the house, set the intention when you first light it that you will continue to burn the candle whenever it is safe with no interruption in the support for your intention.

Simple Intention

Esther Hicks notes that if you can hold a clear intention or desire in your mind uninterrupted for seventeen seconds, it will enter your "vortex" or energy field and be placed in the queue for manifestation when you are ready to vibrate at the level at which it exists. Multiples of seventeen seconds strengthen the intent.

This is one way of thinking about it. At its simple core, the process goes like this:

- Ground, clear, release, and center.

- State your intention: To find work that uses my creativity, passion and skills.

- Meditate on this outcome—visualize it, see it as real, note how it feels, keep it up for as long as you can to form a clear picture in your mind.

- When ready, release it to the Universe/Deity, your Higher Self. State in your own words that you ask for this outcome and that you are placing its completion in the hands of Deity.

As soon as possible, begin to act as if your prayer has been answered in the affirmative.

Chapter Ten

HEALING

You have the power to heal your life, and you need to know that. We think so often that we are helpless, but we're not. We always have the power of our minds . . . Claim and consciously use your power.
—Louise L. Hay

IN PRACTICE, THINGS HAPPEN. There are times things will be going extremely well—the excitement and feeling of accomplishment as you acquire, study, and work with ideas, concepts, practices, and tools that are invigorating and affirming. Divination, manifestation, and ritual will feel deep and fulfilling.

As exciting and motivating as it can be to learn and practice something new, it's necessary to reflect and take time to integrate what you've learned. As adults, we learn by integrating new information with what we already know. So to get the most from all that work, you have to put it aside and allow your mind to make those connections.

Many people lift weights or use other forms of resistance training to build muscle. Resistance training stresses the muscle, but the strength and size of the muscle are actually gained during periods of rest, when the muscle can recover from the strain of lifting weight. So it is with spiritual growth—the actions you take in divination and manifestation will yield information and results, and the actions you take will lead to experiences and learning. But to integrate those lessons, you must have time to rest and recover. I believe that failure to allow recovery and heal the stresses of change is the most significant reason that personal-change efforts fail.

We are spiritual beings having a physical experience. Because both of those things are true, we must maintain balance—we must function in both worlds. We will feel out of balance if we ignore either.

Balancing these aspects requires us to take specific action and care for the priorities in the physical, mental, emotional, and spiritual areas of our lives. "Balance" does not mean continuously devoting 25 percent of our energy to each—it means ensuring that we are maintaining focus on our priorities in those areas and taking appropriate action when necessary.

Any significant change you make in your life will challenge you in all four areas in some way. The most important principle is not to exhaust yourself to the point of stress in any area. Burnout is always a possibility when we are pursuing a goal or making change and feel we are running behind.

Physical Health and Healing

Your physical health and well-being are your foundation—relating to the Earth element, you must be grounded, physically well, and able to do the things required on your path.

The importance of movement (exercise), sound nutrition, water, and rest are well documented and do not need repetition here. However, the following can help you maintain your energy and sense of physical well-being as you begin to make the changes you seek to make:

- *Energy healing*—Acupuncture, Reiki, craniosacral therapy, and many other disciplines are all ways of addressing energetic blockages that manifest as physical symptoms. I strongly suggest you maintain a schedule of regular self-treatment (once you build those skills) and seek practitioners who can support you, and intensify your use of these methods in times of great stress.

- *Mindfulness work*—Using the releasing, grounding, and centering practices mentioned earlier can help you maintain energetic alignment.

Seeking appropriate medical help for your symptoms is most important. The healing practices mentioned above are not intended to be used in isolation—they are complementary practices to other modalities from chiropractic to Western medicine. All disciplines have been developed for a reason. Reiki may help the healing of a broken leg, but the possible surgery and other Western treatment to repair the damage would be necessary.

Mental Health and Healing

The mental challenge is maintaining focus and discipline. Trying to do too many things at once, or mastering a body of knowledge at one sitting, will not be effective. You may recall that, in school, if you left studying for an exam until the last minute and tried "cramming" the night before, you might have passed the test, but you likely forgot most of the content within a few days. To maintain mental resilience, I recommend:

> For every hour you spend on metaphysical subjects, spend an hour on something else. Chunk the material into sections and focus on one at a time, intensively, then leave it alone for a while. The intense effort of focusing will open new pathways in your mind. The period of rest will allow those pathways to connect to prior learning and experience, and you will likely experience "aha" moments when you return to the material. For example, learning the Runes might go like this. Think of these steps as each taking two weeks, with some concentrated time at least every two days:
>
> • Focus on understanding the history, evolution, and the inherent nature and the "why" of the Runes.
>
> • Learn the theme or purpose of each of the three Aetts and why they are associated with Freya, Hagall, and Tir respectively.
>
> • Learn the eight Runes in each Aett and the cycle of manifestation each represents.
>
> • Practice readings on a range of questions so you can learn the interrelationships among them.

Indecision and confusion are also common along this road. Unfortunately, no one outside yourself has the answers. You discussed your purpose and path here with spirit guides and ancestors before you arrived. And so your inner wisdom—consulting your spirit guides and your Higher Self and the Divine—is your best guidance. Whether you use Tarot or Runes, shamanic journey work, or consult another reader or psychic, you will get guidance and suggestions about the conditions facing you and the reasons for them, and sufficient clarity to choose the way forward.

People often wish they were better at time management, but time is not what needs to be managed. We all have twenty-four hours in a day. Our problem is priority management. If we are making changes, that means we must let things go to make room for the new. Most of us had plenty going on in our lives before we started on our path. It is not possible to add water to a full cup. Some will spill out, and it will not be a controlled process. Something is going to have to be released to allow something new to manifest. The good news is you can focus and direct your energy to identify and release those things that are no longer serving you and state your intention to manifest the things you wish to allow to enter your life.

Emotional Health and Healing

As Abraham says, you are supposed to feel good. If you are not feeling good, you are in a state of vibration or emotion that is out of sync with what you are trying to manifest. So your feelings are your best indicator for whether you are following the path to your Soul's evolution that is in your highest good. *A Course in Miracles* notes that fear is the opposite of love. The purpose here is not to go out and acquire love, which is always present. Rather, we need to act to remove the blocks within ourselves to the awareness of the presence of love.

The emotional issues that arise in changing your life may involve feelings of grief and loss for what you are leaving behind, the sadness and perhaps guilt of changing relationships, and the uncertainty and fear that can arise when embarking on a new and unknown direction. To support yourself emotionally, consider these ideas:

- Practitioners who combine energy healing and bodywork with talk and visualization can help you release the emotional blockage and its physical manifestation or symptom simultaneously. Reiki, Bodytalk, craniosacral therapy, neurolinguistic programming, and hypnotherapy are examples of this kind of support.

- Develop a community of like-minded people. Use Meetup.com and other bulletin boards to begin to find groups that resonate with your path and develop relationships that reinforce your direction.

- When you have clearly identified those things that need to be released, conduct a "funeral" for them, which can be as simple as performing a paper-burning ritual as described earlier. Express gratitude for what they contributed to your life, how they were of value, and release them so the energy can be recycled for the good of all.

As mentioned in the section on external resistance, communicate clearly and openly with the important people in your life about what is changing and why. If they are staying in your life, affirm your feelings for them and your desire to stay in a relationship. Ask what they may need from you in the process, in addition to sharing your needs with them. Honor both those staying in your life and yourself during this process.

Spiritual Health and Healing

Maintaining Spiritual resilience is a matter of focus and discipline. The core of our Spiritual path is the purpose and vision we have established for our lives here, and the development of our Souls. To ensure that your will is engaged, make sure to include some form of:

- Daily reaffirmation of your purpose and vision

- Devotion/worship/honoring of the Divine

- Meditation and focus on what you will do today in support of your purpose

- Turning to Divination and therefore inner guidance to determine the cause of any depletion of physical, mental, or emotional energy

- Getting help from others when you don't know what to do next

It is very likely that you will experience physical, mental, and emotional shifts as you pursue your path. Some of these shifts will be welcome flashes of insight. Some will be the emotional and/or physical reaction to seeing things fall away that are no longer serving you.

As these things occur, you may have the urge to abandon or postpone moving forward on your path. But these are the exact moments when you are confronting your "edges"—the areas we discussed as resistance to change.

Hermes Trismegistus brought the principle "as above, so below" from the Vedas to the West—the principle that every atom (the microscosm) holds the universe (the macrocosm) within it and that everything that appears to happen in the physical world happens in the realm of Spirit. Therefore, all of these shifts are happening simultaneously in both. And this also means that you can make a change in either realm, and the change will manifest in the other.

PART THREE

Your Spiritual Growth Plan

Chapter Eleven

FIVE STEPS TO RESUMING YOUR JOURNEY

*In order to carry a positive action we
must develop a positive vision.*
—The Dalai Lama

Step One: Building a Vision

Now that you know where you stand, it's time to craft your vision for your spiritual life and practice. I will ask you to outline the elements of your vision and do some deeper thinking to expand the outline into a vivid story, a clear picture of what your life will be like on this path, and how you will ensure it has "heart."

In this case, the question to be answered is:

What will my life be like when I am fully engaged in the best spiritual path for me? What will I be doing, with whom, and what will I bring into being?

To identify the elements of your vision, use the same tools and approaches that helped you define your starting point.

Approach #1: Go get a reading

Schedule a reading with the reader you consulted in the first exercise if you felt good about that experience, or choose another, offering the question above.

Listen to the recording and summarize the results in your journal.

Approach #2: Three-card or three-Rune reading

The third card or Rune in a past-present-future reading tells you what is likely to happen if you maintain your present course. Meditate on this card or Rune for a while, and use the questions above to define your destination. Note the results in your journal.

Approach #3: Association

Select another image that evokes for you the state you will enjoy when you are fully engaged in your path—pursuing worship, divination, manifestation, in service to your highest values.

Write three things in your journal that made you select this image and use them as a starting point to define your vision for your Spiritual life.

Next, answer the following questions in your journal as well as you can. You may be experiencing some doubt or uncertainty at this point regarding whether you have done everything right, or if you have the strength of will to follow through with your path. Write anyway. We will discuss resistance in a few pages.

Here's an example: The person selected a photo of an arrow in the center of a target as evoking what it will feel like when they are able to manifest and live their path.

Who/what I will be	I am a facilitator, guide, and coach for people seeking to make positive changes in their lives. I am connected with Deity and with my Higher Self through devotions, ritual, and meditation.
What I'll be doing	I am hitting the bull's-eye in every area of my life. I am living a fully present life, choosing words and actions for the good of all. I'm engaged in a mix of activities—writing, teaching, performing, conducting ritual—and working as a teacher, energy healer, and coach/guide to maintain a level of prosperity that enables me to have the positive impact I seek. I practice this process, continually envisioning the next step, acting to make it happen, and using energy healing and divination for reflection and resilience. I have a comfortable home, and I spend time in nature, on the water, and on land.
What I'll manifest	I have built a prosperous spiritual teaching and healing practice that enables me to serve as a facilitator of learning, support, and insight for everyone with whom I come in contact. I experience the richness of connection to Deity through ritual, meditation, and observing the Divine in everything I see. Through forgiveness, I have healed all relationships that can be healed and made peace with the ones that can't.

Step Two: Defining Your Values

What are the values and principles that matter most to you, inspire you, and guide your choices and behavior—the "guardrails" for your life? As we discussed briefly in chapter

1, your values are what you will use to keep yourself on track with your new spiritual path.

There are many theories about how our values develop. Members of the same generation share certain values, which are influenced and affected by significant events in the world at the time they were growing up. Yet, each of us is an individual, seemingly hard-wired to prefer and focus on certain things over others.

Our values are influenced by our families, friends, and personal life experiences. Studies suggest that some are with us from birth and that our mix of values and their relative priority can change over time.

Values can also shift as we mature and grow; we become less inclined to see things in binary, "either/or" terms and more inclined to see others' views as simply different from, but no less valid than, our own. Unhappiness is often due to being required to live and work in a manner contrary to our values. When you discover that your spiritual path is no longer serving you, it is often that your values have shifted, and it is this misalignment that causes the problem.

Our values indicate how we are likely to pursue our vision—the activities we will choose, the outcomes to which we will become committed, and the people with whom we will align.

To me, the most important consideration about the values you serve is that they must be yours. And that you consider the Rede—"Harm none, do as you will."

As we discussed when we reclaimed our spiritual autonomy, living a life that meets someone else's model causes stress at best, disabling inner conflict at worst. And this conflict can result in spiritual, psychological, and physical illness.

It is important to identify your highest-priority values, those you may be over or underemphasizing (and why), and how to renew them as the guiding principles of your life. This is an essential step in building a full life vision to which you can commit, and on which you can follow through. It is my belief that the values listed below, summarized from many sources, represent alternative ways to express love in some form, which is why "love" is not on the list.

A brief taxonomy of values
Using the list below, select for your journal five values that you believe must be served by your time, energy, and commitment. On the page that follows, list those values in terms specific to you and note a few examples of how they must be present in your life for you to feel internal alignment. If something occurs to you that is not on the list, feel free to add it.

Community Family Work/Occupation Relationships Prosperity Service Physical Well-being	Spirituality Independence Connection with Others Creativity Solitude Other Values:

Values and Principles
What will get you across this bridge?

In your journal, create a template like the one below. Now, imagine that you are faced with a long, rickety bridge, on the brink of collapse. It stretches a wide, rushing river, and you know that you must cross it, despite the risk. Write down the values that would provide sufficient motivation for you to cross the bridge. In other words, what are the values for which you would endure significant personal risk?

Once you have chosen the values that would get you across the bridge, add what these values look like in action.

Value: What It Looks Like in Action

1	Being of service	Choosing work that leads to my own and others' growth and development Volunteering in a healthcare organization that promotes healing and compassion
2	Spirituality	Reading uplifting and spiritually enlightening material Participating in ritual and devotions to deepen my relationship with the Divine Practicing forgiveness and compassion for myself and others
3	Achievement	Using my strengths to make things happen for myself and others Achieving sufficient prosperity to allow me to do my work Achieving results that benefit individuals and the community

4	Independence	Being free to manage my own time and energy and work on things that I consider most important
5	Interdependence	Engaging in relationships that provide mutual support and concern for each other's well-being and wholeness Recognizing my impact on others and acting to make it positive

Principles

Next, create a list of five guiding principles—the "rules of the road" for your path based on your values.

For example, I chose the following principles to guide me in the achievement of my vision:

- I seek *engagement with others* to learn and grow through shared experience.

- I seek *solitary time* to integrate my learning.

- I maintain my *physical and mental well-being* to enable me to be of *service.*

- I practice *regular meditation and contemplation* to stay balanced and grounded.

- I regularly *honor Deity* through prayer, ritual, and devotions.

Step Three: Building Capability: What Do You Need?

Having defined your vision and the principles that will guide you as you seek to accomplish it, the next step is to determine whether you have the necessary knowledge and skills to actually bring this vision into being.

The capabilities you acquire or use will be your means to accomplish your vision, the things that will enable action and focus on your spiritual path.

There are two parts to our look at capability. First, consider the elements of your vision for this path and ask yourself the following questions. Journal your responses to refer back to later.

- What attributes or characteristics will you need to express or cultivate in order to achieve your vision?

- What spiritual capabilities—divination, manifestation, psychic skills development—will you need to acquire or strengthen?

- What professional activities will you pursue to express your spiritual path and your values in service?

- What knowledge and skills are required for that work?

- What capabilities do you need to develop or use to ensure that you maintain your spiritual perspective along the way?

There are certain things you may be drawn to—Tarot, crystals, herbs, meditation, energy healing—that you want to develop to an expert level. There will be others that you want to know the basics about but not want to explore the technique as deeply.

The next few pages will allow you to identify the capabilities you need for your next step. You may need to research the answers for the following exercise. For example, if you were to decide that your best expression of your path and values at work is through teaching, you may need to earn a certificate or degree. If you are interested in developing deep expertise in Spiritual counseling, divination, or leadership in a temple setting, you may need to take courses or enter into a structured learning program of another kind.

Before answering the questions, I encourage you to identify the most respected people in the area that interests you and learn how they do it. Then you can identify the core principles that you can use to express and implement your own values and capacities in your own unique way.

Think about the people you know who have achieved a level of fulfillment in a path that appeals to you. Identify one or two of them and, in your journal, describe them as if you were introducing them to someone you know. Write down the answers to the following:

- How does it feel to be around them?

- How would you describe their energy?

- How do they interact with people?

- How do they demonstrate their knowledge and skill?

- How do they live that appeals to you?

- What five words would you use to describe them?

Here's an example:

How does it feel to be around him?
"A" makes me feel safe and as if I am in the presence of someone who could deal with whatever walks through the door. He is serious about serious things but also knows how to joke and laugh and find the irony in situations.

How would you describe his energy?
He radiates strength and solid consistency.

How does he interact with people?
He is careful about whom he takes on as students and clients, but once he commits, he is all in. He is inquisitive—asking questions first to assess your emotional state, then shares the impressions, intuitions, and information he receives to help me make progress. He shows that I always own the next action step.

How does he demonstrate his knowledge and skill?
He manifests what he says he is seeking, or knows the reason why it does not come to pass. I have heard him speak with depth about all aspects of divination, moving energy, and manifestation.

How does he live that appeals to you?
He lives simply and seems to have the ability to want what he has rather than continually trying to get what he wants.

What five words or phrases would you use to describe him?
He is: deeply perceptive, kind, reverent, creative, and an expert.

Do this exercise with two or three people. Then, in your journal, please list the attributes and personal strengths you feel are necessary to realize your vision. They may be ones you identified in thinking about these people, or things that occur to you during your thought process. This exercise with the experts and other people who inspire you is meant to help you brainstorm what aspects and attributes you would also like to possess, but don't be afraid to go off the beaten trail if another attribute occurs to you while doing this exercise.

As you are researching practitioners, experts, and options, use the following framework to record the knowledge and skills you believe are needed to realize your vision.

Using Divination to Identify Necessary Capabilities

The Divination Star is a five-card or -Rune reading that will help you seek inner wisdom regarding the best things for you to learn and acquire to help you on your path. You will be asking the five elements of Spirit (your essential nature), Air (knowledge), Water (emotional strength), Earth (physical tools and skills), and Fire (generating passion and will) for ideas and capabilities that may help you in your journey.

Divination Star
Ground, center, and release.

Invoke spirit guides, Deity, or Higher Self as you wish, to support and help you learn from this exercise.

Clear the energy from your cards or Runes and consecrate them to the task of guiding you in determining what needs to change in each area of the star.

As you consider each question, draw a card or Rune and place it in that position. Note that there are two options for "Air"—you can do both as you wish.

If the card or Rune you draw is ambiguous, or you want more information, ask for what you need (clarification, further knowledge, etc.) and draw another.

Write down the essential meaning of the Rune or card from the materials and how you interpret its significance to you right now.

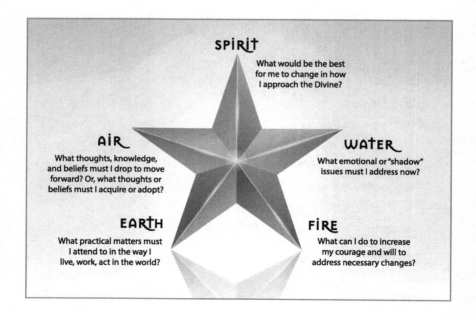

SPIRIT
What would be the best for me to change in how I approach the Divine?

AIR
What thoughts, knowledge, and beliefs must I drop to move forward? Or, what thoughts or beliefs must I acquire or adopt?

WATER
What emotional or "shadow" issues must I address now?

EARTH
What practical matters must I attend to in the way I live, work, act in the world?

FIRE
What can I do to increase my courage and will to address necessary changes?

What are the most important capabilities needed for your vision?

I will realize my vision because I KNOW and PRACTICE	Things of which I need to be aware about the basics and where to find them when needed	Things about which I need sufficient knowledge and skill to use easily	Things I need to know or be able to do well, which I can improvise and vary to suit the situation
The knowledge of concepts, principles, theory Tools and resources (e.g., cards, Runes, crystals, herbs) Other:			
Skills Grounding and clearing energy Focus and concentration Divination Manifestation Ritual Energy healing Other:			

What are the most important resources needed for your vision?

I will realize my vision because I HAVE	
Relationships Support Friendship Love Other:	
Resources Coaches and mentors Friends Finances Other:	

Step Four: Reducing Resistance/ Building Resilience

Chances are the starting point, vision, and values you've identified are not entirely new to you. So what's stopping you from realizing your vision and acting in a manner consistent with your values?

What have you always wanted to do but never did because of fear, self-doubt, or the objections of others? How many plans lie dormant because you could not bring yourself to make them real?

The moment when dreams turn to achievable goals, with mental, emotional, spiritual, and tangible commitment to their success, is the moment when they start to become real. Having defined your vision, your values, the capabilities you need, your strengths and areas for growth, you are close to that point because the next practical step in this process is to create and commit to a plan.

However, when it comes time to commit, you find the promptings of your heart and Soul are edited and blocked by your ego, which employs a range of self-protective strategies or coping mechanisms to keep you safe.

Steven Pressfield provides an outstanding explanation of the role of resistance in his book, *The War of Art*. He notes that resistance to a new way of doing or being arises when:

- The ego is threatened.

- We are preserving some kind of payoff that has become a trade-off—we get something we are afraid to give up but fail to grasp something new.

- We are preserving security and safety, including the safety of preserving the status quo.

- We seek to avoid a frightening risk to our lives or reputation.

But there is value in resistance. Pressfield notes that it comes up only when something important is on the line—so it is a signal that you're getting close to something great. As the Rune Naudiz reveals, the hailstorm or test of confronting resistance serves as a means to get stronger—or not—and it can sharpen your focus for disciplined action. It also serves as a test for whether you are truly committed to your values, goals, and beliefs.

Internal resistance

Each of us has a couple of inner voices that talk to us about our nature, our capabilities, our worth, and our likely success. One of those—which many psychologists have termed our "inner critic"—likes to warn us when we are getting close to the brink of change. Some of us even know the name of this critical inner voice. This is the voice that has been warning you throughout this book that you are in dangerous territory—that the safe routes to spiritual growth have all been mapped, and personal experience can't be trusted.

This is the voice of resistance. I wrote a song about it that goes like this:

When the going gets easy,
That's when the hard part begins.
Some of us can't stand the peace
When we run out of battles to win.
When there's no limit to freedom,
When the pain truly lives in the past,
Part of you strives to keep your worries alive
Because you know good times never last.

The harder the road, the more surely you know
That your life is being fulfilled.
You'll create as much pain as you need to contain
That dangerous joy that's within you.

There are many things that your critical inner voice may say to you that will block you from pursuing your new Spiritual path. They may be either the voice of fear or the voice of someone who cautioned you never to appear unusual or draw attention to yourself. Someone who said to set your priorities by completing what you *have* to do before you do what you *want* to do and other such rules that keep you securely in their comfort zone. Those people may be gone now, and if they aren't, you might want to consider whether they should be. But their voice lingers as your critical inner voice.

For the sake of your Spiritual autonomy, it is important to differentiate between your own inner guidance and the leftover judgments from prior times.

Use the following framework to identify the most limiting, damaging messages you get from your inner critic. Identify the message, who's speaking, and the impact on you.

Your Critical Inner Voice: What Is It Saying?

	THE MESSAGE	WHO'S SPEAKING?	IMPACT ON YOU
About you			

	THE MESSAGE	WHO'S SPEAKING?	IMPACT ON YOU
About your plans			
About others in your life			

Managing the Critical Inner Voice

This discussion of inner resistance is crucial to your success, because if you succumb to the limitations imposed by this voice, you will lose momentum and perhaps even give up from a belief that "resistance is futile" and change is impossible.

But there is another voice inside us—the one that encourages us, affirms our value, and feels joy in our success. Many of us have a hard time hearing this voice consistently—it may get loud enough when we have had enough of the inner critic. When you are standing at the top of a zip line, it is the critic that yammers about the risk and possible catastrophe awaiting you. It is the constructive inner voice that gives you a metaphysical shove and sends you on the ride of your life. The song I quoted above ends with the inner "coach" saying:

Take the time that you need now.
Don't let anyone stand in your way.
Let the Souls that you're saving take care of themselves

For at least the next couple of days.
You've earned a personal sunrise.
And there's a message in the morning light.
There's a part in this show that was written for you,
And only you can play it right.

Any coach supports their "client" by observing and reflecting back what they do; finding patterns in what works and what doesn't; gathering and communicating credible, meaningful, and accurate feedback; and praising accomplishment. Then they help you look for ways to build on that accomplishment to continue your progress toward your vision. We each need to be able to do this for ourselves to at least the same degree that we listen to our critical inner voice.

That said, think about a time when someone has praised you in very vague and general terms, that showed they really didn't know you or what they were talking about. This is not coaching. And in "coaching yourself," positive thinking alone won't do it.

Affirmations can be a useful tool as you are learning to be your own inner coach, as they provide opportunities for focus and contemplation. But they should be yours, affirming the presence of things in your life that you are trying to manifest. Quite simply:

- Focus and contemplation result in making a vision that you want to see achieved.

- Your vision guides you in planning how to achieve your goal.

- Planning leads to action.

• Action leads to results.

And results—success in reaching the milestones you set for yourself—are the source of your affirmations and the content of your inner coaching dialogue. There is no better affirmation than "I did it before, I can surely do it again."

Use the space below to list the things that your constructive inner voice is telling you about your strengths, your value, your support, and your possibilities.

What Your Constructive Inner Voice Says about Your Gifts and Strengths:

	THE MESSAGE	WHO'S SPEAKING?	IMPACT ON YOU
About you			
About your dreams			
About others in your life			

Using Constructive Inner Messages

In your journal, note one inner-critic message that particularly gets in your way. Note what your inner coach would likely have to say about it. And in the third box, write an affirmative statement about your value, your worth, your capability, or your likelihood of success that you can use whenever the inner critic pipes up.

This will provide the opportunity to shed light on the shadows that hide your inner critic. Identify the damaging statements and beliefs your inner critic maintains and tell the real story.

External Resistance

In one sense, all resistance is internal. It is either our inner dialogue that trips us up, or the way we react to external events. But there are three ways to deal with stress we experience from others—we can get out of the situation, we can remove the stressor from the situation, or we can change our reaction.

Sometimes, we may be living or working with people whose energy conflicts with what we are trying to accomplish, and we don't want to leave, we don't want them to leave, but we can't change our reaction, because it is rooted in one of our core values. For example, your attempts to be authentically peaceful and centered can be derailed by an environment full of negativity and critical judgment.

Using this process, you are likely to be changing your routines and the way you live your life in some way. For those around you who have "figured you out" and become accustomed to your current way of living, change in someone they have known and depended on for a long time can be threatening. They may try to get you to go back to the way you were.

In your journal, please identify the external conditions that will need to be released or created to support you in your vision. Specifically:

- To what extent do you need to change your environment?

- How will the "new you" evoke reactions from others?

- From whom?

Managing External Resistance: Negotiating Change

The first decision about external resistance is whether to retain those relationships or release them.

If you choose to retain them, it means you care about them, and their continued presence in your life is important to you. So it will be necessary and worth your time and effort to talk about what you're doing and why and the role you would hope they would play in your life.

Resistance to this idea is frequently based on the fear that if they know the truth, they will reject you. And honestly, that is a risk because they, too, are autonomous Spiritual beings.

But demonstrating their importance to you by engaging in this conversation is, in itself, a relationship-building experience.

The formula that follows can help you prepare for this conversation. There are six key elements to the conversation:

1. Describe where you are going—your vision—
   and why.

2. Explain why it's important to you and the values that drive you.

3. Test for understanding: Ask what the other
   person has heard you say and correct any
   misperceptions.

4. Describe what the change will mean for your
   activities and your presence.

5. Describe what you want—their continued
   support, friendship, etc.

6. Inquire: Ask what they need from you.

You can use this template for building a conversation about change in the relationship dynamics your new commitment will cause.

I would suggest that you journal on each of these components, so that you can have a good idea in your head of what you would like to say to this person—or you can even read your answers to them directly from your journal if you feel comfortable doing that. It can be helpful to have your words planned ahead of time, especially if you feel you will be meeting with great resistance or negativity.

Step Five: Create Your Plan

It is time to pull all the previous four steps together into a path forward. The pages that follow are your resources for confirming your commitment to your vision for your path and your most deeply held values. It's important to refine this now and ensure that your desire and commitment to this new direction are clear.

Next, you'll identify the capabilities you need to start working on now—and your plan for doing so. This is the step that begins to build momentum, to get you moving down the road you have chosen.

Finally, you'll identify the specific actions to take and how you will know if you are succeeding.

On the next page, begin by envisioning the successful completion of your plan—what will it be like to get there?

The outcomes I'll experience

Journal on the following questions to see what it will feel like when you reach your goals:

- What will I be celebrating?

- What will my spiritual practice look like?
  What will I be doing regularly?

- What places will work and relationships have
  in my life?

- What will be getting my time and attention?

Your path forward

Taking only sixty seconds to do so, journal the main essence of your vision. You can use this as a "mission statement" to look back on to help you answer the next set of questions.

- What are the values that will be served by this
  vision?

- What are the strengths I already have that will help me get there?

- What capabilities do I need to realize my vision? And to what extent do I currently demonstrate them?

- What personal attributes and characteristics do I need to demonstrate? To what extent do I currently demonstrate them?

Finally, list the actions you will take and the resources you can consult to move forward with your plan. You can use the chart below as a template.

My Next Steps

OBJECTIVE	ACTIONS	RESOURCES	DATE
To sustain my commitment			
To manage my internal resistance			

OBJECTIVE	ACTIONS	RESOURCES	DATE
To manage external resistance			
To build knowledge and skills			

Who's Coming with You?

Anyone contemplating significant change in the way they see and navigate their world must consider how it will change their lifestyle. And one of the biggest questions we ask in this life is who will be with us.

There are many people who practice a rich internal spirituality on their own—many books have been written about solitary Wiccan practice, for example. The implications for others in your life would be different if you wished to be active in a temple or group of some kind. In the case of the solitary practice, working with the external-resistance model in the previous section will help you ensure that you can put the right boundaries around your practice and have support for doing so. To join a group may mean withdrawing time from others presently in your life, and so you may find yourself releasing some people from your world.

In your journal, identify some learning partners in this journey—people in whom you can confide, who can help in a range of ways. The key questions to ask yourself as you journal about these people are:

- Who is supporting you?

- How can they help?

- How can you reciprocate?

CONCLUSION

IF YOU HAVE DONE the exercises and the reflective work in the preceding pages, you have likely already worked your way through the first five cards of the Major Arcana.

Like the Fool, you have trusted in the Divine and yourself sufficiently to embark on a new path or a new leg of your current journey.

You have drawn on the energy of the Magician/Magus to develop your communication skills with Spirit through Divination—asking for and learning to listen for guidance. You have also increased your magical abilities through manifestation, both in creating your vision and plan and in using the tools and practices we discussed.

Using the energy of the High Priestess, you have identified your core values and the principles that will guide you on your path—what you will and won't do, the ethical perspective of the Law of Three, and to do as you will so long as it harms none.

In your assessment of your capabilities, and building the core skills covered here, you drew on the power of the Empress to translate the spiritual, ethereal knowledge and information into action—brought it from "above" to "below."

And finally, the Emperor card energy has led you to a written plan and strategy for moving forward that integrates Spirit and matter.

Now comes the doing.

It has been my intention to support your healing, learning, and growth through sharing my own experiences and learning, and pointing you toward those with depth and breadth greater than mine in all these subjects.

The process you have worked through to define and embark on your new spiritual direction can also be used for other forms of manifestation, growth, and change. It is also entirely possible, even likely, that you may find yourself in the future at a similar point that made you pick up this book in the first place. You now have a process you can reach for and use to save yourself time:

- Build your vision

- Define (or redefine) your values

- Build your skills

- Reduce resistance

- Create your plan

For small things, it involves simply being clear about your need, developing a vivid picture of what you want, consulting your values for guidance, using divination and manifestation techniques as support, and acting as if it has been answered by moving forward with a plan of action. But on the larger journey question, I would like to leave you with the following statement from The Charge of the Goddess, read at most Full Moon rituals.

> Therefore, let there be beauty and strength, power and compassion, honor and humility, mirth and reverence within you. And you who seek to find Me in the depths of the sea or the shining stars, know that your seeking will avail you not unless you know the Mystery. For if that which you seek you find not within yourself, you will never find it without. For behold—I have been with you from the beginning and I am that which is attained at the end of desire.

Self-Initiation

It is very likely that a teacher will appear now. As described in nearly every introduction to Wicca or Paganism, I suggest you perform a self-initiation to honor your completion of these preparatory steps.

Find a peaceful time and place where you will not be disturbed for at least half an hour. Collect your journal, a pen, and a white candle.

- Center, ground, and release excess energy.

- Light your candle.

- Imagine a circle of light forming around you, protective and supportive.

- Invoke whichever supportive Spirits and Divine Helpers you have learned to know.

- Write for at least ten minutes, describing your intention to follow through on the plan you have created, and realize your vision. I share with you my own, below:

I recognize tonight that this is one, connected Universe, created by the Goddess and the God who are themselves the Creation of the One Creator. I am one with all things, and all things are one with me. I am loved, blessed, and welcomed by the Goddess and the God, and I seek to grow and learn and follow this path with care, love, and sovereignty.

I seek the freedom of mind, heart, body, and Spirit to do as I will, as long as I harm none.

I seek the power, tools, and understanding to fulfill my mission and purpose for this life.

I seek insight, spiritual vision, and power to accomplish good works, to be useful while here and worthy of relationship with the Divine.

I seek to love and be loved, to be connected, and to experience the feeling of being home.

I seek to live a praiseworthy life in the time that remains to me, not for others' praise, but to die knowing I was worthy of having lived.

I seek the lessons that will bring me closer to the Goddess and the God, and the will and skill to master them.

I will follow this path because it has heart. I will integrate all I have experienced and learned before.

I will live as an inspirer, teacher, friend, and leader to help others find their path home.

May the Goddess and the God see and accept me as I am, help me grow into what I will be, and show me the way.

Merry Meet, Merry Part, Merry Meet Again.
May You Blessed Be.

BIBLIOGRAPHY

Cosmology

Foundation for Inner Peace. *A Course in Miracles.* New York: Penguin Books, 1975–1996.

Renard, Gary R. *The Disappearance of the Universe.* New York: Hay House, 2004.

Divination

Arrien, Angeles. *The Tarot Handbook: Practical Application of Ancient Visual Symbols.* New York: Tarcher/Penguin, 1997.

Bunning, Joan. *Learning the Tarot.* San Francisco: Weiser Books, 1998.

Khatwani, Munisha. "22 Major Arcana Cards in Tarot." YouTube, 2009.

Peschel, Lisa. *A Practical Guide to the Runes.* Woodbury, MN: Llewellyn Worldwide, 2007.

Thirteen. "Thirteen's Tarot Card Meanings." www.Aeclectic. net, date unknown.

Thorsson, Edred. *Futhark: A Handbook of Rune Magic.* San Francisco: Weiser Books, 1984.

———. *Runelore.* Boston: Weiser Books, 1987.

———. *Runecaster's Handbook,* San Francisco: Weiser Books, 1999.

Tyriel. *The Book of Rune Secrets*. Vancouver, BC, Canada: Rune Secrets, 2012.

Waite, Arthur Edward. *The Pictorial Key to the Tarot*. Stamford, CT: US Games Systems, Inc., 1971.

Healing (also see Shamanism)

Baginski, Bodo, and Shalila Sharomon. *Reiki: Universal Life Energy*. Mendocino, CA: LifeRhythm, 1988, 2004.

Dey, Eileen. *Touching the World Through Reiki*. Bothwell, WA: Book Publishers Network, 2010

Krieger, Dolores. *The Therapeutic Touch: How to Use Your Hands to Help and Heal*. New York: Simon and Schuster, 1979.

Stein, Diane. *Essential Reiki*. Berkeley, CA: Crossing Press, 1995.

Manifestation

Bonewits, Isaac. *Real Magic*. Boston: Weiser Books, 1989.

Hicks, Esther, and Jerry Hicks. *Ask and It Is Given*. Carlsbad, CA: Hay House, Inc., 2004.

Shamanism

Castaneda, Carlos. *The Teachings of Don Juan: A Yaqui Way of Knowledge*. Berkeley, CA: University of California Press, 1969.

Harner, Michael. *The Way of the Shaman*. New York: Bantam Books, 1982, 2006.

Meadows, Kenneth. *Urban Shaman*. Great Britain: Element Books Limited; Rockport, MA: Element Inc., 1991.

Wicca and Paganism

Buckland, Raymond. *Buckland's Complete Book of Witchcraft*. Woodbury, MN: Llewellyn Publications, 2002.

Cabot, Laurie. *The Power of the Witch*. New York: Bantam Doubleday Dell, 1989.

Cunningham, Scott. *Wicca: A Guide for the Solitary Practitioner*. 40th printing. Woodbury, MN: Llewellyn Worldwide, 2007.

Leland, Charles Godfrey. *Aradia: Gospel of the Witches, 1899*. EZREADS.Net, 2009

Lewis, Rev. Donald. *Lessons in the Correllian Tradition. First Degree*. Woodbury, MN: Llewellyn Worldwide, 2008.

―――. *Lessons in the Correllian Tradition, Second Degree*. Woodbury, MN: Llewellyn Worldwide, 2008.

―――. *Lessons in the Correllian Tradition, Third Degree*. Woodbury, MN: Llewellyn Worldwide, 2008.

Tompkins, Debbie. *Living the Wiccan Life*. Woodbury, MN: Llewellyn Publications, 2009.

Zimmerman, Denise, and Katherine Gleason. *The Complete Idiot's Guide to Wicca and Witchcraft*. 2nd ed., New York: Alpha (The Penguin Group) 2003.

Personal and Psychological Growth and Change

Bridges, William. *Managing Transitions*. Cambridge, MA: DaCapo Press, 2004.

Conway, Flo, and Jim Sigelman. *Snapping: America's Epidemic of Sudden Personality Change*. 2nd ed., New York: Stillpoint Press, 1995.

Crace, R. Kely, and Duane Brown. The *Life Values Inventory* material. http://www.lifevaluesinventory.org/, 2012

Kopp, Sheldon. *If You Meet the Buddha on the Road, Kill Him!* Palo Alto, CA: Science and Behavior Books, 1972.

Kübler-Ross, Elisabeth. *On Death and Dying.* New York: The Macmillan Company, 1969.

Loehr, Jim. *The Power of Story.* New York: Free Press (Simon and Schuster) 2007.

Mackenzie, Gordon. *Orbiting the Giant Hairball.* New York: Penguin Group, 1998.

Ralston, Peter. *The Book of Not Knowing.* Berkeley, CA: North Atlantic Books, 2010.

Scherer, John. *Work and the Human Spirit.* Spokane, WA: John Scherer and Associates, 1993.

———. *Five Questions That Change Everything.* Fort Collins, CO: Bibliocast, 2011.

Senge, Peter, et al. *Presence.* New York: Doubleday, 2004.

Stone, Hal, and Sidra Stone. *Embracing Your Inner Critic: Turning Self-Criticism into a Creative Asset.* New York: HarperCollins Publishers, 1993.